Antonín Dvořák
on Records

ANTONÍN DVOŘÁK ON RECORDS

Compiled by John H. Yoell

Discographies, Number 46

GREENWOOD PRESS
New York • Westport, Connecticut • London

Library of Congress Cataloging-in-Publication Data

Yoell, John H.
    Antonín Dvořák on records / compiled by John H. Yoell.
      p.   cm.—(Discographies, ISSN 0192-334X ; 46)
    Includes indexes.
    ISBN 0-313-27367-7 (alk. paper)
    1. Dvořák, Antonín, 1841-1904 – Discography.   I. Title.
  II. Series.
  ML156.5.D9Y6   1991
  016.78'092—dc20   91-24038

British Library Cataloguing in Publication Data is available.

Library of Congress Catalog Card Number: 91-24038
ISBN: 0-313-27367-7
ISSN: 0192-334X

First published in 1991

Greenwood Press, 88 Post Road West, Westport, CT 06881
An imprint of Greenwood Publishing Group, Inc.

Printed in the United States of America

∞™

The paper used in this book complies with the
Permanent Paper Standard issued by the National
Information Standards Organization (Z39.48-1984).

10 9 8 7 6 5 4 3 2 1

Contents

Foreword

During the preparation of a new, thoroughly revised edition of the Antonín Dvořák Thematic Catalogue, it was decided not to include a part of the first edition, namely the Discography, since the size of the new catalogue, as large as it will appear now, would exceed any reasonable measure. And, this is also important, the users of a discography may not be, in many cases, so seriously interested in the whole bulk of other Dvořák matters, and vice versa. (Fields of specialization, whether we like it or not, keep one another apart.)

Thus it became urgent -- to collect and publish a special book containing dependable and encompassing information on the huge field of this modern and important medium of presenting music -- to publish a Dvořák Discography.

November 1987 saw a special exhibition organized in Prague with the theme DVOŘÁK AND THE WORLD OF GRAMOPHONE RECORDING. In introducing it, I expressed the opinion that Dvořák, who was always so interested in every modern technical device (not out of naivety but in testimony of his alert mind), would certainly enjoy the unforeseeable development of this medium, which in his own day was not much more than a child's toy. (By the way, we have tried searching for the phonograph cylinders in which his voice apparently was caught during his presence at the Chicago World's Fair in 1893!)

Since the beginning of the stormy evolution of recording, Dvořák's compositions were objects of that process. This Discography mentions samples of those works. In the course of the past ninety years, innumerable recordings of Dvořák's works have been issued, especially of his symphonic works. At the time of the aforementioned exhibition, five complete editions of his nine symphonies were presented. As for individual works, the Ninth, "The New World", had 127 recordings; the eighth 47; the seventh 25; and so on. Moreover, the concertos found a vivid interest: the Cello Concerto had 56 recordings; the Violin Concerto 30; and the Piano Concerto 14 recordings. The two series of <u>Slavonic Dances</u> complete were available in seven interpretations of the orchestral and in eight of the original piano-duet versions.

In the chamber music field the winners are, naturally, the string quartets. There exists an enormous number of individual recordings. At the head is the "American" op.96, followed by the more profound ones -- the G and A flat major.

In this way we could continue, but it would be unnecessary to forego what the reader of this Discography can easily find himself (not to mention the evident fact that what I reported in the year 1987 is certainly antiquated by today's facts).

This book has, however, another important goal: it can demonstrate to the world's recording companies which fields of Dvořák's oeuvre are still less frequented, and where are the lacunae which should be filled in, evident especially in Dvořák's vocal work, including operas. Whereas we have several recordings of the more popular items, <u>Rusalka</u>, there are precious works having none.

It can be hoped that the Sesquicentennial Celebrations of Dvořák's birth will offer a welcome opportunity to fill these gaps and to present music -- not only to Dvořák fans -- in new, exciting performances covering both the most popular and most neglected parts of his musical estate. May this book help to achieve that end.

Jarmil Burghauser
Prague

Acknowledgments

Of persons contributing to <u>Antonín Dvořák on Records</u>, special gratitude goes to K. Kokot, Neutral Bay, Australia, who proved tireless in submitting listings and in manuscript review. Further, deep appreciation goes to Markéta Hallová, Dvořák Society, Prague, for her valuable suggestions and determination in ferreting out the earliest Dvořák recordings. To Jarmil Burghauser, nestor of Dvořák scholars, goes credit not only for suggesting the discography project, but also for standing by it at critical junctures. And gratitude to Barbara Sawka, who extended ideas along with courtesies at the Stanford Archive of Recorded Sound, as did staff at the Czech Music Fund and Antonín Dvořák Museum.

Wayne Shoaf, Nick Strimple, Eric Hughes, Michael Gray, Harry Butler, Václava Benešová, Alan and Lucinda Houtchens, and Annette and Louis Kaufman are gratefully remembered for their interest.

At the production and editorial end, thanks go to the patient Mary M. Blair at Greenwood Publishing Group, while Jan Claire Elliott, Dorothy H. Thomas and Mark E. Heidmann lent their skills to manuscript preparation, assisted by support from the Association of Recorded Sound Collections (ARSC). Without these persons and institutions the project could not have reached completion.

The book further owes its existence to Marilou, who gave up many evenings and weekends to the clatter of the typewriter. And, amazingly enough, she still enjoys Dvořák!

Preface

The selective discography <u>Antonín Dvořák on Records</u> offers an itemized perusal down the composer's works list which should prove useful to collectors, practicing musicians, teachers, librarians, disc jockeys, sales personnel, record company representatives -- anyone who loves music and relates to it in recorded form. No spacious account of recorded Dvořák has appeared since 1960, when Otakar Svoboda appended a list of recordings to the first edition of Jarmil Burghauser's <u>Antonín Dvořák Thematic Catalogue</u>. What amounted to a large number of recordings on 78 rpm and early LP has since turned into a tidal wave.

While an exhaustive Dvořák discography tracking down every scrap of music from the composer's workbench might be possible given generous time, much money and access to current computer technology, the need for this Herculean task is less acute than a collector's roundup of memorable records from the past geared into what has been issued since the advent of compact discs (CD). What might be considered the greening of Dvořák on records began with the introduction of the LP, and despite areas of unevenness the discography has become amply if not ideally representative of the great Czech master.

Since the mid-1980's the chief thrust of the record industry has shifted to digital methodology and settled on the compact disc as the new international norm. This revolution has added new luster to Dvořák's full-blooded music which benefits so much from enhanced, detailed sound reproduction. Old recordings, even from the acoustic days, take on new life when transferred to the digital format. So the pragmatic decision was made to confine the present survey to selected LPs and CDs which most fully encompass the vast pool of recorded Dvořák. Other modalities, for instance cassette tape and the video disc, constitute ancillary convenience.

Antonín Dvořák ended his distinguished career a complete composer, very much in touch with the most eminent musicians of his time down through the broad mass of ordinary listeners and amateur performers. His work has never gone out of style; the capacity of generations to absorb and perpetuate certain pieces like the "New World" Symphony or Cello Concerto in B Minor shows no sign of abatement. These are among the most popular concert items in existence with recordings now numbering into the hundreds. And the public has come to appreciate Dvořák's mastery of composition in all the accepted forms including opera, chamber music, song and works of sacred purpose. In all these areas Dvořák has left a lasting mark. His fund of ideas can appear limitless, which astonished even the likes of Brahms. Yet the misconception persists that Dvořák was some sort of supremely gifted peasant shaking spontaneous creation from his sleeve. In the light of present-day scholarship, this view can be dismissed as sheer nonsense.

Dvořák mastered his craft slowly and after dogged struggle; while the habit of jotting musical ideas on his cuffs could sometimes create a laundry problem, like most composers he worked mainly from sketch books. A thorough professional born out of the Bohemian cantorial tradition, Dvořák was sufficiently ambitious to break out of his milieu from time to time to personally plant seeds on receptive foreign soil, notably Britain and the United States, as the solid underpinning for his international reputation. The 150th Anniversary of his birth marks a good time to revaluate Dvořák's role as an artist and explore the further reaches of his creative genius. The availability of recordings is an obvious prime tool for that purpose.

If nothing else, the present discography aims to bring home the diversity and overall excellence of Dvořák's art as documented on a host of recordings from many nations. If interest can be piqued in the unfamiliar sides of Dvořák, and fresh respect generated for his established masterpieces, then this listener will consider his goal achieved.

Introduction:
Overview of Historical Recordings

By living only four years into the 20th Century, Antonín Dvořák easily can be forgiven for not having judged the full implications and potential of the phonograph, which would become the major channel for passing his music on to other generations. But given his intense interest in things mechanical, notably a passion for locomotives and steamships, it seems difficult to believe that he could remain oblivious to sound recording. By the time Dvořák died, Edison's invention as modified by Emil Berliner was rapidly advancing beyond the stage of a mere child's toy. Yet, according to staff at the Antonín Dvořák Museum, no talking machine or recordings form a known part of the Czech master's legacy.

Lack of information about Dvořák's reaction (if any) to recorded music is curious. By 1899, the London-based Gramophone Company had initiated recording sessions in major Continental cities including Vienna and Budapest; Prague was not far behind. Soon both Columbia and Pathe were reaching out to the Habsburg lands. Appreciation of the Slavic market came early; the extent of the Russian vocal catalogue remains one of the wonders of early operatic discography. Singers at Prague's National Theater were recording too, bringing selections from Czech operas to records including items by Dvořák.

The rumor about Dvořák recording his voice in Chicago awaits the presentation of evidence. More surprising is no Dvořák recording among the known cylinders cut by Gianni Bettini, who maintained a studio in New York when Dvořák was a resident in the city, expressly to capture voices of the musically famous.

There is, however, one feeble clue that Dvořák might have participated in the mechanical reproduction of his music -- one Antonin Dvorak is catalogued as the performer of <u>Humoresque</u> on a Duo-Art piano roll (No. 0538). This listing, however, could be a case of mistaken identity since Marie Dvorak, the composer's niece, did make several piano rolls for the Aeolian Company including works by her celebrated relative. No disc transfers of this highly interesting material are known.

Who was the first artist to record Dvořák? Precise information is not at hand, but a spurt of interest appeared just after the premiere of <u>Rusalka</u>. Vilma Hajková (a member of the original cast) cut the scullion's aria from Act III, a precious cylinder said to lie somewhere inside the technical museum in Prague. Previously, on 31 March 1901, tenor Bohumil Pták faced the horn to record one of the Prince's arias from <u>Rusalka</u>, a dim, distant presence which can be heard today in LP transfer in Supraphon album "100 Years of Opera at the National Theater" (a set of five discs, nos. 1016 3741/46). In this treasure-trove Karel Burian, Žiková and other vintage voices from the Golden Age of the National

Theater sing again from <u>Dimitrij</u>, <u>Šelma sedlák</u>, <u>Armida</u> and other Dvořák operas. There is also an excerpt from the oratorio <u>Saint Ludmila</u> by Dvořák's favorite soprano Růžena Maturová (the first Rusalka and Armida). Another prominent singer, sometimes known as the "Czech Caruso," tenor Ottakar Marák did not neglect Dvořák in the course of a stream of recordings. His voice survives on at least two LP transfers, Supraphon 0 12 1509 and Court Opera Classics CO-367.

By the year of Dvořák's death foreign recordings of his music begin to be noticed; for example, early English cylinders by singer Ben Davies in "Songs my mother taught me," and Marie Hall (a pupil of Ottakar Sevčik) playing the violin in an arrangement of <u>Humoresque</u>. About the same time, Fritz Kreisler had started to record his various arrangements of Dvorak which attained great popularity.

Bohemia's eminent violinist Jan Kubelik recorded much, but his contribution to the Dvorak discography seems limited to <u>Humoresque</u> (Supraphon 1011 3193).

Singers reigned supreme in the early years of acoustic recording. Neither the technology nor the public were then available for extended excursions into chamber or symphonic music. This helps to explain why so much important Dvořák lagged in coming to records.

Among celebrity singers who gave Dvořák some attention was Emmy Destinn, a staunch Czech patriot who recorded extensively for Odeon, Columbia, Victor and other major labels. Her "Lieblicher Mond" from <u>Rusalka</u> (Victor 88519) remains a classic often repeated on LP (Scala 804; O.A.S.I. 603). She also recorded a few of Dvořák's songs.

Nellie Melba supplied Victor with at least two accounts of the ubiquitous "Songs my mother taught me." One was with orchestra (88483), the other with Frank St. Leger as accompanist (88535), a version not released but subsequently available in private issue (Stanford Archive of Recorded Sound StARS 1000). There may have been an even earlier recording, from 1913, released as HMV DB 356 (Pearl GEMM 9353).

Dvořák's popular art song attracted further famous singers, among them Geraldine Ferrar (Victor 87350) and Hulda Lashanka (Columbia 77719). Perhaps the first to record the complete cycle <u>Gypsy Songs</u> was soprano Zdenka Krausova in 1929, shortly before recording by the vertical cut method was discontinued (Pathe X 5051/53).

Until Gaspar Casado with the Berlin Philharmonic under Schmidt-Isserstedt delivered a complete Cello Concerto (Telefunken E 1893/97), the piece had been represented as excerpts in acoustic sound, for example as played by Emanuel Feuermann (Parlophone E-10482). But in 1928 this cellist committed the full score to discs supported by the Berlin State Opera led by M. Taube for

Parlophone/Columbia (CD reissue Chanterelle HS-2001). This pioneer version is not to be confused with Feuermann's much later performance in New York, since brought live to CD (Philips 420 776-2). As for Dvořák's symphonies, it is no surprise to find the highly successful "From the New World" first on discs. Ten sides were cut at the Free Trade Hall in Manchester in 1924 by the enterprising Hamilton Harty with the Hallé Orchestra. This was released on English Columbia (9770/74; Masterworks Album 77). Soon after, Landon Ronald delivered a second version for HMV with the Royal Albert Hall Orchestra (album 43). Around this time, of course, Leopold Stokwoski in the United States was gearing up for his famous recording of the symphony subsequently released as Victor Album M-1.

For the G Major Symphony (today numbered the Eighth), the earliest appearance on discs seems to be Basil Cameron conducting unspecified players on Brunswick 30125/28.

Meanwhile, Leopold Stokowski had begun to flex the muscles of his formidable Philadelphia Orchestra in Victor's studios at Camden, New Jersey. Takes of the "Largo" from the "New World" Symphony came as early as 1917, although not released; then a more successful try in 1921 released by Victor as 74631. In 1925, at the dawn of electrical recording, Stokowski felt ready to record the entire symphony with various substitutions in the instrumentation. Finally, in 1927, the persistent maestro did it: the first recording of a full symphony by an American orchestra on native soil. Known to generations of discophiles as Victor Album M-1 (LP reissue RCA CRL2-0334), this milestone incited controversy, as did much else performed by Stokowski on or off records. Heard today, his flamboyant, indulgent mannerisms are obvious, yet the stamp of a remarkable conductor is unmistakable.

Although Stokowski recorded Dvořák's most popular symphony many times over with various orchestras, he remained curiously detached from most of the Czech master's other music, even when recording with the Czech Philharmonic (one Slavonic Dance excepted). In the early 1970s, however, Stokowski "discovered" the Serenade in E Major, and left a ravishing account of it on Desmar 1011.

Electrical recording eventually expanded representation of Dvořák's chamber music, previously confined to isolated movements. There were, however, acoustic versions of the celebrated "American" String Quartet, for example, by the Bohemian Quartet with Dvořák's son-in-law Josef Suk on second violin (Vox 665/67). This was joined in 1926 by the Budapest String Quartet recorded electrically (Victor M-14; CD reissue Novello Records NVLCD 903). Other early landmarks were an uncut "Dumky" Trio from the Budapest Trio on Brunswick, while a recording of the great Piano Quintet, op.81, actually goes as far back as 1911 with the Rosé Quartet. One of Artur Schnabel's rare excursions into the

Dvořák repertoire took place in 1934 when he joined the Pro Arte Quartet for opus 81 (Victor M-219; CD reissue Arabesque 26613).

The 1930s witnessed maturation of the gramophone industry inside the newly-formed Czechoslovak Republic. This territory had long been cultivated by complex subsidiaries of the international combines including the Gramophone Company, whose ubiquitous canine trademark translates into Czech as Hlas jeho pána. Newer recording technology brought formation of a German-Dutch enterprise issuing discs in Czechoslovakia under the Ultraphon label. Rapid expansion brought financial reverses leading to acquisition by Telefunken, yet the Ultraphon label remained highly visible prior to World War II.

Closer to home was the Prague-based firm Esta (derived from the name of founder Emil Star). Founded in 1928, Esta eventually fell under control of the native publishing house Melantrich. With musical matters managed by the energetic Jan Seidl (also a composer), Esta set about recording much Czech classical music. By 1931 the Czechs had become major exporters of gramophone records, as they are today.

Under the guiding hand of conductor Václav Talich, a solid exponent of the Czech nationalist school, the resources of the Czech Philharmonic were brought to bear on records. By the close of the 1930s Talich had bolstered the Dvořák discography with landmark releases of the Sixth and Seventh Symphonies, a supple Eighth and the complete Slavonic Dances. These received broad circulation on the HMV and Victor labels, and now are being welcomed back on compact discs. Talich's younger colleague, George Szell, presided over the disc debut of the Czech Philharmonic in the "New World" Symphony. Talich's associate conductor, František Stupka, also did much to help bring the Czech Philharmonic to its level of pre-war excellence. His recordings are comparatively few, but Stupka's energetic conducting of Dvořák's last two symphonies is vivid (Panton 01 0447/8).

A telling episode in gramophone history arrived in April 1937, when the indomitable Fred Gaisberg dispatched a British team to Prague expressly to capture Pablo Casals performing Dvořák's Cello Concerto with Szell conducting the Czech Philharmonic. Crossing the tense German-Czech frontier in a train virtually empty, Gaisberg reached Prague just in time to catch the recording session. The atmosphere must have been electric because Casals outdid himself in a monumental performance matched by conductor and orchestra (HMV album 306; EMI Angel/Reference CDH 7 63498-2). Like Bruno Walter's account of Mahler's Ninth Symphony with the pre-Anschlus Vienna Philharmonic, Casals' legendary recording survives as a precious memento of music-making in mid-zone Europe as once it was.

The young Yehudi Menuhin, backed by the Paris Conservatory Orchestra under his teacher Georges Enesco, seems to have been first in committing Dvořák's Violin Concerto to discs in 1936 (HMV DB 2838/41; LP reissue EMI/HMV Treasury EH 749395). Although Menuhin went on to a distinguished career both as violinist and conductor, Dvořák's music does not loom large on his list of priorities.

For all his tinkering with the Slavonic Dances and other items, the failure of Fritz Kreisler to record the Violin Concerto seems strange. Although well-known in the concert world at the turn of the century, this work only came into its own on discs after the LP revolution, through soloists like Nathan Milstein, Josef Suk and Isaac Stern, among others. The remarkable Jascha Heifetz had recorded minor Dvořák pieces as early as 1919, yet he too bypassed the Violin Concerto. His main thrust towards Dvořák came in the 1960s with chamber music, notably the Piano Trio in F Minor, op.65 (CBS Masterworks Portrait MP 38781), the "Dumky" Trio (RCA LSC-3068) and the Piano Quintet, op.81 (RCA/Gold Seal 7965-2).

Sir Thomas Beecham, a true friend of the gramophone, could remember when Dvořák was still composing and formed early affection for the Czech master's music. What he chose to record, however, tended to be unconventional: Slavonic Rhapsody No. 3, one of the Legends and the Symphonic Variations, all on Columbia when these pieces were still unrecorded or rare on discs. Beecham may have been the first conductor to record a full symphony concert on magnetic tape, an experiment when he took the London Philharmonic on tour of Nazi Germany in 1936. This historic tape apparently no longer exists, but Vernon Handley has repeated the entire program (including the Dvořák Eighth Symphony) as a tribute to Beecham's memory (Chandos DBT 2007 S). Beecham, however, did leave another account of the Eighth Symphony on records with the Royal Philharmonic (Odeon ALP-2003; EMI CDM 7 63399 2).

At a time when few batons waved over Dvořák's late tone poems, the testy Sir Thomas would place pieces like The Golden Spinning Wheel on his programs. In 1947, he recorded this onetime rarity (EMI/ Retrospect Series SH 1003). Beecham's total of recorded Dvořák is meager, but he did break new ground. Like Stokowski, he was an erratic yet dedicated Dvořákian.

One of the most durable of all conductors, Arthur Fiedler led the Boston Pops Orchestra in countless recordings over a fifty-year span. These include one of the earliest recordings of the Hussite Overture (Victor 12-0234/35; LP reissue RCA LM 1) as well as accounts of the Carnival Overture. Fiedler's rendering of Dvořák's Ninth Symphony with the Boston Symphony Orchestra still stands above a very crowded field as a recording of true distinction (RCA/Papillon 6530-2-RG).

Another conductor with long tenure and a long list of recordings, Eugene Ormandy and the Philadelphia Orchestra contributed several versions of Dvořák's last three symphonies for Columbia and RCA. In the 1930s, Ormandy was one of the first to record Scherzo capriccioso, while a truly scarce item is "Dr. Eugene Ormandy" as solo violinist recording Humoresque back in 1926 (Romeo 243). The reliable Ormandy further presided at the conductor's desk for recordings of the Cello and Violin Concertos.

The deteriorating situation in Europe during the 1930s and 1940s meant an influx of musical talent to the United States. The cream of the refugee conductors-- Bruno Walter, Fritz Reiner, Pierre Monteux and Erich Leinsdorf -- carried on into the LP era to enrich the catalogue with standard Dvořák items, delivered from time to time. Leinsdorf, however, proved more adventurous with his presentation of the Sixth Symphony in D Major (then known as the First) (Columbia ML 4119).

In 1946, George Szell came to the Cleveland Orchestra to build in the heart of America an organization close in style to the Czech Philharmonic. For Epic and Columbia, Szell systematically traversed the core Dvořák repertoire: the last three symphonies, complete Slavonic Dances and the Carnival Overture; there also was a Piano Concerto with Firkusny. Szell's recipe for solid musicianship and precision playing is hard to surpass, and these performances linger in circulation. Regrettably, Szell at Cleveland did not explore Dvořák's list of works more widely.

The year 1941 marked the 100th Anniversary of Dvořák's birth, but this coincided with possibly the lowest point in Czech history. Not only was Hitler's swastika fluttering over Prague Castle, but his most sinister henchman, Reinhard Heydrich, had come to the city to formulate plans for the eventual extermination of the Czech people. Curiously, these dire portents did not mean an automatic ban on Dvořák's music. The centennial, as much as possible, was observed with special concerts and opera performances, although in virtual isolation.

Wilhelm Furtwängler apparently conducted Dvořák's "From the New World" Symphony for the occasion at Prague Castle, a bizarre tribute if true. A subsequent recording of this symphony (but not the actual performance), dated 1941, has surfaced on which the eminent German maestro allegedly leads the Berlin Philharmonic (Relief 813; AS DISC AS-111). This seems to be spurious, the duplicate of a 1944 recording with the Munich Philharmonic under Oswald Kabasta (Royale 1257). So crediting Furtwängler with any recordings of Dvořák's music rests on shaky ground. His younger colleague Herbert von Karajan, however, registered the first of several "New World" Symphony recordings as far back as 1940 (Deutsche Grammophon 423 528-2). After the war Karajan regularly delivered Dvořák symphonies and other works in Berlin and Vienna.

Despite enormous difficulties as the flames of war engulfed Europe, the production of records continued in Germany and what was left of the Czechoslovak Republic. The tenacity of firms like Telefunken, which shifted personnel and presses from place to place as the war hit home, is astounding. The high quality of German recordings, which included magnetic tape, could only be appreciated after hostilities had ceased.

Following the collapse of the Third Reich, one of the first priorities in liberated Czechoslovakia was to restore the Czech Philharmonic to full strength, notably under the younger conductors Raphael Kubelik and Karel Ančerl. Both participated in fresh recordings with the orchestra, but departed before their work was complete. Kubelik, especially developed most of his career abroad as he continued to record Dvořák, including a complete cycle of the symphonies and the Erben tone poems for Deutsche Grammophon.

Although Václav Talich experienced postwar political difficulties, he did manage to contribute significant entries to the Dvořák discography during his final years. These included tone poems and retakes of the Slavonic Dances. Other conductors, like Václav Smetáček who directed the Prague Symphony Orchestra, came on the scene to make notable additions to the previously meager representation of Dvořák's major choral works.

Directly after the war, Esta, Ultraphon and other parts of the earlier Czech recording industry were nationalized to form the new entity Supraphon. As far as Dvořák is concerned, the Supraphon product remains indispensable. Two other labels, Panton and Slovakia's Opus, later arrived to augment the country's strides in documenting Dvořák.

Looking back over a century of recording art, the legacy of Antonín Dvořák has fared well. As for all classical composers, advances in audio technology, mass marketing and corporate mergers continue to exert a profound effect on the availability and reissue of given recordings, as well as the direction new production will take. With all the changes in the sociology of music, opportunities to become familiar with Dvořák's music on an intimate level have never been better. Whether or not this means Dvořák eventually will be considered an important -- as opposed to merely likeable -- composer only time will reveal. But recordings remain the deciding factor. Of this reality, there can be no doubt.

Abbreviations

s = soprano

a = alto

t = tenor

b = bass

mz-s = mezzo-soprano

c = contralto

mz-c = mezzo-contralto

ba = baritone

b-ba = bass-baritone

v = violin

va = viola

vc = cello

db = double bass (string bass)

qt = quartet

stg = string

ens = ensemble

hm = harmonium

hp = harp

p = piano (pianoforte)

f = flute

tu = tuba

cond = conducted by

rec = recorded

arr = arranged

rev = revised

orch = orchestrated

ov = overture

O = Orchestra

PO = Philharmonic Orchestra

SO = Symphony Orchestra

Cz = Czech

E = English

G = German

DGG = Deutsche Grammophon Gessellschaft

ASV = Academy Sound and Vision

MHS = Musical Heritage Society

RCA = RCA (Victor Records)

CBS = CBS (CBS Records)

CD = compact disc; indicated by asterisk (*)

LP = long-play (33 1/3 rpm) disc; no asterisk

Discography

I

Works for the Stage

ALFRED. Heroic opera in three acts (B.16)(1870). Libretto by Karl Theodor Körner.

* Records International 7013-2. Slovak Philharmonic Orchestra conduct Libor Pešek (+ Vanda; Šelma Sedlák overtures; Rhapsody). *Overture only*

KING AND CHARCOAL BURNER (Král a uhlíř). Comic opera in three acts.

Version I, op.12 (B.21)(1871); Version II, op.14 (B.42)(1887)

Libretto by Bernard Guldener (B.J. Lobeský)

* Marco Polo 8.223272. CSSR State Orchestra (Košice) conducted by Robert Stankovsky (+ opera overtures and preludes). *Overture only*

THE STUBBORN LOVERS (Tvrdé palice). Comic opera in one act, op.17 (B.46)(1874). Libretto by Josef Stolba

Said to bubble over with charming music, Dvořák's short comedy has won scant attention on or off records.

VANDA. Tragic opera in five acts, op.25 (B.55)(1875; rev 1879 and 1883). Libretto by František Zakrejs and Václav Beneš-Sumavský.

Supraphon 10 4071-1 602 (106 4071/72). Tikalová; Petrová; Kalaš; Blachut; Bednář; Rujan; Jankovský; Hanzaliková; Prague Radio Chorus; Prague Radio Orchestra conducted by František Dyk. Rec 1951.

* Records International 7013-2. Slovak Philharmonic Orchestra conducted by Libor Pešek (+ Dramatic Overture; Šelma Sedlák; Rhapsody). *Overture only*

An ambitious historical saga about a Polish princess who ultimately drowns herself in the Vistula to save her country, Vanda juxtaposes a patchwork libretto against impressive musical realization, especially in the choral department. Collectors owe Supraphon a debt of gratitude for releasing this archival material, even if in monaural sound and heavily cut. The overture, composed later than the opera, makes a worthy concert item.

THE CUNNING PEASANT (ŠELMA SEDLÁK). Comic opera in two acts, op.37 (B.67)(1877). Libretto by Josef Otakar Vesely.

> Supraphon 1116 4931/33. Zítek; Depoltová; Berman; Soběhartová; Vodička; Kundlák; Prague Radio Chorus; Prague Symphony Orchestra conducted by František Vajnar.

> * Records International 7013-2. Slovak Philharmonic Orchestra conducted by Stephen Gunzenhauser (+ Vanda; Dramatic Overture; Rhapsody). *Overture only*

Also known in English as The Scheming Farmer or The Peasant a Rogue, this work marks Dvořák's first unqualified success in the opera house. Here he challenged Smetana on home ground.

Supplementary Recording:

> Panton 8016 0157. Teodor Šrubař (b); Prague Radio SO/Dyk. Count's aria from Act I only.

DIMITRIJ. Historic opera in four acts, op.64 (B.127 and 186)(1882; rev 1885, 1895). Libretto by Marie Cervinková-Riegerová.

> Supraphon 1116 3040. Přibyl; Beňačková-Čapová; Dvořáková; Randová et al; Prague Radio Chorus; Prague Radio Symphony Orchestra conducted by Jan Štych. Rec 1980. *Highlights*

> * Marco Polo 8.223272. ČSSR State Orchestra conducted by Robert Stankovsy. *Overture.*

Dvořák's plunge into ancient Kremlin power struggles deals with an amalgam of historic events closely connected to Mussorgsky's Boris Godounov. Radical revision bent Dimitrij in the direction of Wagnerian music drama, creating serious problems whenever the opera goes onstage. Supraphon's highlights offer a compromise between two competing versions. The resulting impression is an opera perhaps best appreciated for vivid dramatic scenes and colorful Slavic choruses.

Supplementary Recordings:

Supraphon DM 1001. National Theater O/Vogel. *Overture* (ten-inch LP)

Supraphon O 12 1579. Dimitrij's aria from Act I "Bud žehnán, slávy naší památníku." Karel Burian (t) in "Karel Burian Operatic Recital."

Supraphon 1 12 1809. Dimitrij's aria from Act II "Z divokého žití viru." Vilém Přibyl (t) in "Vilém Přibyl Opera Recital". Supraphon 1116 2536 in "Antonín Dvořák Opera Scenes".

BASF/Merian 98 22181-4. Dimitrij's aria from Act III. Bogdan Paprocki (t) in "Prag: Die Meister der Tschechischen Oper" (eight LP)

Supraphon DV 6099/SV 8237 in "Recital of Slavic Opera."

Note: In 1989 a recording of the entire original version took place in Czechoslovakia for Supraphon, conducted by Gerd Albrecht. Commercial release remains to be confirmed.

THE JACOBIN. Opera in three acts, op.84 (B.159 and 200)(1888 rev 1897). Libretto by Marie Červinková-Riegerová.

Supraphon 1112 2481/83. Zítek; Machotková; Průša; Berman; Blachut; Šounová; Přibyl et al; Kantilena Children's Chorus; Kühn Mixed Chorus; Brno State Philharmonic Orchestra conducted by Jiří Pinkas.

ProArte PAD 3000.

Despite the title, politics color Dvořák's seventh opera only in the ill-will between a prodigal son (returning from revolutionary Paris to his Bohemian birthplace) and his stuffy, aristocratic father. Subplots deal with lovers' misunderstandings. At the core of the opera is Benda--village schoolmaster and model of an old-time Bohemian musician. Dvořák's endearing projection of Benda doubtless reflects fond memories of his own teacher--Antonín Liehmann. The heartwarming opera makes a plea for sane, sensible family and human relationships borne by Dvořák's mature, tuneful idiom.

Supplemental Recordings:

Supraphon LPV 1139. Soloists, Chorus and Orchestra of the Prague Smetana Theater/Vogel. *Highlights*

BASF/Merian 98 22181-4 (eight LP)

Supraphon 1116 2536. Terinka's aria from Act II "Na Podzim v oreši." Nad'a Šormová (s); National Theater O/Kuchinka.

Supraphon 1116 3256. Count's aria from Act III "Ten úsměv děcka." Jaroslav Horáček (b); Prague Radio SO/Vajnar in Jaroslav Horáček operatic recital.

* Marco Polo 8.223272. ČSSR State Orchestra/Stankovsky. Preludes to Acts I and II; Ballet music from Act III.

THE DEVIL AND KATE (CERT A KACA). Opera in three acts, op.112 (B.201)(1889). Libretto by Adolf Wenig

Supraphon 1116 3181/83 (10-3181-1 613). Barová; Novák; Ježil; Šulcová; Horáček et al; Brno Janáček Opera Chorus and Orchestra conducted by Jiří Pinkas.

Lacking the element of love interest, plot for The Devil and Kate focuses on the social problems of a gawky, talkative spinster with a consuming passion for dancing. Kate, one of the more curious heroines in all opera, unwittingly tumbles down to hell where she proves too much for Lucifer. In Act III she trounces him again, saving a princess from his clutches and correcting labor abuse in the bargain. Kate ends up with a mansion and lifetime supply of dancing partners. By bringing in modified lietmotiv technique to fortify the wacky plot and characters, Dvořak merges voices, dances and orchestral substructure into a seamless, unified whole. Dance episodes, used not as balletic adjuncts but as integral parts of the work, turn The Devil and Kate into a dance opera with few peers.

Supplementary Recordings:

Supraphon DV 5303/05. Havlák; Komancová; Kočí; Krilová; Asmus et al; Chorus and Orchestra of the National Theater/Chalabala (three LP)

Artia ALPO 81

Telefunken SAT 22506. Leipzig Gewandhaus O/Neumann. *Dance in Hell; Prelude to Act III only* (+ Smetana; Janacek)

Panton 11 0284. Czech PO/Neumann. Prelude to Act III only in "Famous Opera Overtures"

* Marco Polo 223272. ČSSR State O/Stankovsky. *Overture; Preludes to Acts II and III; Infernal Dance from Act II*

RUSALKA. Lyric fairy tale in three acts, op.114 (B.203)(1900). Libretto by Jaroslav Kvapil.

* Supraphon C37 7201/03 (10 3641). Beňačková-Čapová; Ochman; Soukupová; Jonašová et al; Prague Philharmonic Chorus; Czech Philharmonic Orchestra conducted by Václav Neumann (three CD)

* Supraphon/Crystal 11 0617-2 *Excerpts*

Supraphon 10 2641 633 (1115 3641/3)(three LP)

As an opera composer, Dvořák scored his greatest success with <u>Rusalka</u>. The original fable may have Slavic roots, but many pens in many languages have brought focus, refinement and fresh twists to this legend including several operas. What makes the Czech master's treatment stand out from antecedents is his musical response to a well-written libretto which echos Dvořák's own consistent convictions about nature, love and life. His ability to convey empathy for the doomed heroine in her half-lit, watery other-world stands as a remarkable artistic achievement. Rightly, <u>Rusalka</u> has taken its place among the top showpieces of Czech opera, a work of vast appeal and uncommon value.

<u>Supplemental Recordings</u>:

Supraphon DV 5118/21. Červinková; Haken et al; Chorus and O of National Theater/Krombholc (four LP)

Supraphon DV 5864/67 (SV 8049/52; 50440/43). Šubrtová; Haken et al; Chorus and O of National Theater/Chalabala

Artia ALPO 89

Supraphon 50802. *Excerpts*

Urania US 5219. Frick; Trotschel et al; Dresden State Opera Chorus; Saxon State O/Keilberth (G)(three LP)

Eurodisc 201 599-250. Bindszus; Adam et al; Chorus of German State Opera Berlin; Die Staatskapelle Berlin/Apelt (G). *Excerpts*

BASF/Merian 9822181. Soloists, chorus, O of National Theater/Krombholc (Cz) in "Prag Die Meister Der Tschechischen Oper" (eight LP). *Excerpts*

<u>Rusalka's Song to the Moon from Act I</u>: "Měsíčku na nebi hlubokém;" "Du lieber Mond, so silberzart;" "O, moon high up in the deep, deep sky."

* EMI CDC 7 49319-2. Lucia Popp

EMI 7 49319-1

* Acanta 43326. Lucia Popp

* Philips 422 073-2. Karita Mattila

    Philips 422-073-1

* Supraphon CO-1970 (10 2843-2 611) Gabriela Beňačková-Čapová

    Supraphon 1116 2843

* Melodram MEL 26511. Ljuba Wellitsch

* Encanto END 5201. Pilar Lorengar

    London SO-26381 (25995)

    Decca SPA 578 (SXL 6267)

Electrola 057-46 116. Annliese Rothenberger

Rodolphe Productions RP 12401. Teresa Zylis-Gara

London SR 33192. Inge Borkh

Opus 9012 0971/72. Stefania Hulmanová (two LP)

Scala 804. Emmy Destinn (from Victor 85519, 78 rpm, rec 1915)

Rubini GV 28. Ada Nordenova (from HMV AN 319, 78 rpm)

Pearl GEMM 261/2. Jarmila Novotna

* Legato Classics LCD 126-1. Aprile Millo. Rec 1986

DGG 136 011. Rita Streich

RCA ARL1-2529. Leontyne Price

RCA/Victrola 1198. Zinka Milanov

Muza SX 1114. Teresa Wojtaszek Kubiak

Incantation of the witch Jezibaba from Act I: "Čury mury fuk."

    Supraphon 1116 2696. Eva Randová

    Supraphon 116 2536. Milada Šubrtová

    Opus 9112 0414. Ljuba Baricová

Opus 9012 0971. Helena Bartošová

<u>Prince's aria</u> from Act I: Vidino divná, přesladká"

    Supraphon 1 12 1164. Ivo Žídek

    Supraphon 1116 2536. Jiri Zahradníček

<u>Prince's aria</u> from Act I: "Ustante v lovu"

    Supraphon 1 12 1809. Vilém Přibyl with Josef Klán

<u>Prince's aria</u> from Act I: "Vim, ze jsi kouzlo"

    Opus 9112 1262. František Livora

<u>Ballet Music</u> (Polonaise) from Act II

   * Philips 422 3872-2. Czech PO/Neumann (+ Cello Concerto)

   * Opus/Allegro 9150 1189. Radio Bratislava SO/Lenárd (+ Polonaise in E-Flat; Tchaikovsky et al) in "Famous Orchestral Polonaises"

    Panton 8110 0319. Czech PO/Neumann (+ Fučík et al). In "Little Pearls of Czech Classics." Rec 1983

<u>Watersprite's Aria</u> from Act II "Celý svět nedá te"

    Supraphon 1116 3156. Jaroslav Horáček (b) in opera recital

<u>Watersprite's Aria</u> from Act II "Květiny bílé po cestě

    Supraphon 1116 2536. Eduard Haken (b) in "Antonín Dvořák: Scenes from the Operas"

Act III, Final Scene

    Panton 8116 0347. Hajóssyová (s); Přibyl (t); Novák (b); Czech PO/Neumann. Rec live at House of Artists, Prague, 1983. In "Czech Philharmonic: National Theater"

<u>Rusalka's</u> <u>aria</u> from Act III "Necitelná vodní moci"

> Supraphon 1116 2536. Milada Šubrtová (s) in "Antonín Dvořák: Scenes from the Operas"
>
> Opus 9012 0971. Helena Bartošová (s) in "Z Historie Opery" (two LP)

<u>Aria</u> (unlisted in catalogue). Opus 9356 2023. Peter Mikuláš (b)

<u>Note</u>: For a complete <u>Rusalka</u> on video disc see RM Arts RU502, an English National Opera production conducted by Mark Elder, recorded in 1986. A live concert production in New York 5 June 1987 has been captured on audio cassette by Lyric Distribution Inc. as ALD-1352. No LP or CD counterparts to these performances are known.

*   Marco Polo 8.223272. CSSR State O/Robert Stankovsy. *Overture; Polonaise*

ARMIDA. Opera in four acts, op.115 (B.206)(1902). Libretto by Jaroslav Vrchlický

*   Foyer 2015. Caballé; Schlott; Ruesche; Scheibner; Orchestra and Chorus of the Bremen City Theater conducted by Alexander Albrecht. Rec 1961 (two CD)

> VOCE-2 (two LP)

<u>Armida's</u> <u>aria</u> from Act I "Za štíhlou gazelou"

*   EMI 7 49319-2. Lucia Popp (s) in "Slavonic Opera Arias"

*   Supraphon 10 2843-2 611. Gabriela Beňačková

> Supraphon 1116 2843

    For his last major work, Dvořák settled on one of the most shopworn topics in all opera--the trials and tribulations of the Crusaders as given in Tasso's epic poem <u>Jerusalem Delivered.</u> Gluck, Handel, Rossini and at least 50 other composers have based operas on this material. In Dvořák's case, he seemed determined to come up with a Czech equivalent to Tannhäuser, but things misfired at the premiere; the Prague audience turned thumbs down, delivering a bitter blow to the composer. Rightly or wrongly, the fortunes of <u>Armida</u> have been dismal ever since.

    The initial recording on VOCE/Foyer, heavily cut and sonically substandard, was taken from the first performance ever given outside Czechoslovakia when Montserrat Caballé was starting her international career. If nothing else, <u>Armida</u> offers a juicy title role, so a first-class recording might give this languishing epic of duty, love and self-sacrifice a new lease on life.

<u>Supplementary Recordings</u>:

> Supraphon DM 1001. National Theater O/Vogel. *Overture* (+ Dimitrij Overture) (ten-inch LP)

> * Marco Polo 223272. ČSSR State O/Stankovsky. *Overture* (+ Overtures and Preludes)

JOSEF KAJETÁN TYL. Overture and Incidental Music, op.62 (B.125) (1881; rev 1885, 1895)

Besides the Overture--better known as <u>My Home</u>--Dvořak's contribution to a play about Bohemia's esteemed dramatist J.K. Tyl (1808-1856) is otherwise limited to a pair of intermezzi plus dramatic music to accompany each act. Evidently no modern recording documents the complete score.

See Overture *My Home*

II

Oratorios, Cantatas, Masses

HYMNUS; THE HEIRS OF THE WHITE MOUNTAIN, op.30 (B.27). Poem by Vitĕzslav Hálek. (1871; rev 1884)

* Supraphon CDS-7230. Czech Philharmonic Chorus; Czech Philharmonic Orchestra conducted by Václav Neumann (+ Psalm 149; Te Deum)

   Supraphon 1112 3577 (ProArte PAD 112 3577)

Hálek's poem, reinforced by Dvořák's solemn music, dwells on past national humiliation, but offers hope for the continued integrity of the Czech people. In this work Dvořák tasted his first public success as a composer.

Supplementary Recordings:

   Supraphon 1 12 1437. Czech Philharmonic Chorus; Prague SO/ Košler (+ Smetana; Foerster) in Czech Classic Cantatas

STABAT MATER, op.58 (B.171)(1877)

* Supraphon CDS-7378/79. Beňačková; Wenkel; Dvorský; Rootering; Czech Philharmonic Chorus; Czech Philharmonic Orchestra conducted by Wolfgang Sawallisch. (two CD)

   Supraphon 1112 3561/62

   ProArte 2PAD-209

   DMM Ariola-Supraphon 302 187-435

* Vienna Master Series CD 160 104. Jeric; Houska; Novsak; Reja; Petrusanec; Chamber Choir of Radio Television Ljubljana; Mixed Choir Obala Koper; Consortium musicum; Radio Symphony Orchestra Ljubljana conducted by Marko Munih.

   * Royal Crown Classics CD 65105 (+ Largo from Symphony No. 9) *Excerpts*

The Stabat Mater helped promote Dvořák's name abroad, especially in England. A basic lyric impulse guides this music, the directness and poignancy tinctured by the composer's personal heartache over the loss of three infant children in rapid succession. Dvořák on Calvary was not an armchair witness.

Supplementary Recordings:

Supraphon DV 5212/13. Soloists, chorus, Czech PO/ Talich. Rec 1952

Artia ALP 182/83

Urania URLP 234

Colosseum 162/63 (+ Symphony No. 9)

Rediffusion Heritage Collection HCN 8011/12

Ariola-Eurodisc XC 26 199K

* Pilz PLZ-104. Soloists; chorus; Munich Radio SO/Marko

DGG 138 818/19. Soloists, chorus, Czech PO/ Smetáček (two LP)

DGG 2707 014. Soloists, chorus, Bavarian Radio SO/Kubelik (two LP)

 * DGG 413 688-2. "Virgo virginum praeclara" only. In "Ave Maria" (+ Bach et al)

Melodia/Chant du Monde LDX 78729/21. Soloists, chorus, Leningrad PO/Tchernouchenko (two LP)

Vox SVUX 52020. Soloists, chorus, Westphalian SO/Reichert (two LP)

PSALM 149, op.74 (B.154)(1879; rev 1887)

* Supraphon CDS-7230. Czech Philharmonic Chorus; Czech Philharmonic Orchestra conducted by Václav Neumann (+ Hymnus; Te Deum)

Supraphon 1112 3577 (1C 3577-1 231)

ProArte PAD 155

"Sing to Jehovah a new song," the Old Testament psalmist proclaimed; Dvorak, once a church organist, obliges with an extended hymn in resounding C major. The revised version for mixed choir and retouched orchestration (originally op.52 for male choir with orchestra) lets Dvořák open all stops with Handelian exuberance.

Supplementary Recordings:

> Schwann Musica Sacra AMS 89. Czech Philharmonic Choir; O of the
> Czechoslovak Radio Bratislava/Smetáček (+ Te Deum; Saint Ludmila finale;
> Caldara)
>
> Supraphon/Master Series MS 0981-2. Czech Philharmonic Chorus; Prague
> SO/Smetáček (+ Mass in D; Te Deum; Biblical Songs) (two LP)

TE DEUM, op.103 (B.176)(1892)

* Supraphon CDS-7230. Beňačková-Čapová; Souček; Czech Philharmonic
  Chorus; Czech Philharmonic Orchestra conducted by Václav Neumann (+
  Hymnus; Psalm 149). Rec 1984

> Supraphon 1112 3577
>
> ProArte PAD 155
>
> DMM/Ariola 206718-425
>
> Ariola-Eurodisc LP 610279

The rousing Te Deum served as Dvořák's calling card when he first set foot in the
New World.   Whether or not he consciously worked American Indian musical
elements into the score is not entirely clear, but the opening measures hammered out
as if by frantic tom-toms does come across as primitive stuff. When focus shifts to
the soloists the piece settles down to the ebb and flow of the Latin text. Exuberance
returns for a final, ecstatic Alleluia.

Supplemental Recordings:

> Schwann Musica Sacra AMS-89. Solosits, chorus, Prague SO/Smetáček
> (+ Psalm 149; St. Ludmila finale; Caldara)
>
> Supraphon MS 0981-1. Prague SO with soloists and chorus/Smetáček (+ Mass
> in D; Psalm 149; Biblical Songs. (two LP)

THE SPECTER'S BRIDE, dramatic cantata, op.69 (B.135)(1884). Ballad after Karel
Jaromír Erben

> Supraphon 10 8038-1 212 (50381/82). Tikalová; Blachut; Mraz: Czech
>   Philharmonic Chorus; Czech Philharmonic Orchestra conducted by
>   Jaroslav Krombholc
>
> Artia ALP-196

*   Urania US 5161-CD. Czech Philharmonic Orchestra conducted by Jaroslav Krombholc (+ Water Goblin; Hussite; Smetana). *Prelude* only

The macabre subject--a suitor's decomposing corpse returns to claim his bride--unwinds over a sometimes awkward and repetitious text minutely followed by the composer. Yet this large-scale choral work is more than a quaint Victorian heirloom. The composer holds interest by means of ingenious orchestral touches and lucid choral writing. Sheer craftsmanship saves this spooky narrative from its literary deficiencies, letting it emerge as a unified musical whole.

THE AMERICAN FLAG. Patriotic cantata, op.102 (B.177)(1892). Poem by Joseph Rodman Drake

> Columbia M 34513. Evans; McDaniel; St. Hedwig's Cathedral Choir; Berlin Radio Symphony Orchestra conducted by Michael Tilson Thomas(+ American Suite)

In The American Flag Dvořák competently responded to a commission from Mrs. Jeannette M. Thurber, his ambitious and persistent New York patroness. Significantly, he failed to remain a few extra days in the city to attend the first performance. The bellicose doggerel handed him as a text (penned during the War of 1812) turns patriotism into embarrassment.

SAINT LUDMILA. Oratorio, op.71 (B.144)(1886). Libretto by Jaroslav Vrchlický

> Supraphon 10 8180-1 213 (SUA ST 50585/87; DV 6064/66; SV 8180/82) Zikmundová; Soukupová; Blachut; Krejčík; R. Novák; Czech Philharmonic Chorus; Prague Symphony Orchestra conducted by Václav Smetáček (three LP)

A venerable set has survived several editions of Supraphon's catalogue to document the grandest of all Dvořák's choral enterprises, and a true landmark in Czech music. The oratorio largely follows the British tradition laid down by Handel and Mendelssohn, although the subject is the mythical story of how Christianity came to Bohemia. Dvořák indulges in a sumptuous celebration of the Slavic spirit, and passages invoking nature belong to the finest ever drawn by the Czech master. In Part III he hits full stride with a virile setting of the ancient Czech hymn "Lord have mercy."

Supplementary Recordings:

> Schwann Musica Sacra AMS 63 (AMS 2563). Soloists; chorus; Prague SO/ Smetáček (+ Foerster; Micina; Office from Kiev et al). *Finale only*

> Schwann Musica Sacra AMS 89. Soloists; chorus; Prague SO/ Smetáček (+ Psalm 149; Te Deum; Caldara). *Finale only*

MASS IN D MAJOR, op.86 (B.175)(1887; rev 1892)

* Carus 83.106 CD. Hein-Guardian; Kelber; Janzen; Hein; Jorg Zettler (o); Mottetchor Stuttgart conducted by Gunter Graulich. Original version

* Preiser 93378. Schmid; Bernheimer; Reinprecht; Sramek; Ullmann (o); Choir and Orchestra of St. Augustin Vienna conducted by Friedrich Wolf. Revised version. Rec 1987

* Koch-Schwann 113 008FA. Tikalová; Mixová; Blachut; Haken; Vachulka (o); Prague SO FOK/ Smetáček. Revised version

    Schwann Musica Sacra AMS 29

    What might be considered the little brother of Dvořák's mighty Requiem, the Mass in D dutifully proceeds through the Roman service in a devout, often disarming way. Composing on commission to consecrate a private chapel, Dvořák originally scored for modest forces--soloists, choir and organ. Later he delivered the concert version employing full orchestra.

Supplementary Recordings:

    Supraphon/Master Series MS 0981/82 (1112 0981/81). Machotková; Skatulová; Lindbauer; Jedlička; Tvrzský (o); Prague SO/ Smetáček (+ Te Deum; Psalm 149; Biblical Songs). Revised version

    Argo ZRG 781. Soloists; Choir of Christ Church Cathedral Oxford; Cleobury (o)/ Preston. Original version

REQUIEM MASS, op.89 (B.165)(1890)

* Supraphon C 37-7427/28. Beňačková-Čapová; Fassbaender; Moser; Rootering; Czech Philharmonic Chorus; Czech Philharmonic Orchestra conducted by Wolfgang Sawallisch (two CD)

    Supraphon 10 4241-1 232 (1112 4241/42) (two LP)

* London 421810-2. Lorengar; Ilosfalvy; Krause; Ambrosian Singers; London Symphony Orchestra conducted by Istvan Kertesz (+ Kodály) (two CD)

    London OSA 1281 (two LP)

* Opus 9356 1883/84. Hojóssyová; Soukupová; Kundlák; Mikuláš; Slovak Philharmonic Orchestra conducted by Zdeněk Košler (two CD)

The Requiem looms like a cathedral arch above all Dvořák's church music. Compared to the operatic tendencies of Verdi or Berlioz, Dvořák moderated the fire and brimstone implicit in the Mass for the dead to offer music reflecting deeply-felt trust in God as the merciful redeemer. A unifying four-note motto theme runs through the entire work in various guises. Particularly thrilling is the close of the Offertorium, a grand fugue on the words "quam olim Abrahae."

Supplementary Recordings:

Supraphon 1112 2216/17. Soloists, chorus, Czech PO/Ančerl (two LP)

Supraphon SUA ST 50057/58

DGG 2707005

Erato STU 71430. Soloists, chorus, ORTF O/Jordan (two LP)

III

Works for Orchestra

Integrated Sets: Symphonies 1-9 (1865-1894)

* DGG 423-120-2. Berlin Philharmonic Orchestra conducted by Raphael Kubelik (+ Carnival; Wood Dove; Scherzo capriccioso) (six CD)

    DGG 2720 066-10 (nine LP), symphonies only

* London 417 598-2. London Symphony Orchestra conducted by István Kertesz (+ Symphonic Variations) (seven CD)

    Vox Box SVBX 5137; 5138; 5139 (+ overtures etc) (nine LP)

    Supraphon 1 10 1621/28 (10 1621-1 018). Czech Philharmonic Orchestra conducted by Václav Neumann (eight LP)

    Opus 9110 1421/18. Slovak Philharmonic Orchestra conducted by Zdeněk Košler (eight LP)

SYMPHONY NO. 1 IN C MINOR, op.3 (B.9) (1865), "The Bells of Zlonice"

* Supraphon CO-2143. Czech Philharmonic Orchestra conducted by Václav Neumann. Rec 1987

* Chandos CHAN-8597. Scottish National Orchestra conducted by Neemi Järvi (+ Heroic Song)

    Chandos ABDR -1291

The hefty, long-mislaid First Symphony only resurfaced in 1923, and is particularly interesting as a very early Dvořák orchestral score in pristine condition, unretouched or revised. Despite a surplus of sober symphonic ideas, sometimes not completely digested, logic and structural coherence endure.

Supplementary Recordings:

Supraphon DV 5373. Prague SO/Neumann. Cut version

Artia ALP 140

London CS 6523/CM 9523. London SO/ Kertesz

Decca/Jubilee KJBC 110

Opus 9110 0993. Slovak PO/ Košler

MHS 824-824 Y (+ Symphony No. 2) (two LP)

Philips 6500 122. London SO/ Rowicki

SYMPHONY NO. 2 IN B-FLAT MAJOR, op.4 (B.12) (1865)

*   Denon CO-2253.   Czech Philharmonic Orchestra conducted by Václav Neumann

*   Chandos CHAN-8589. Scottish National Orchestra conducted by Neeme Järvi (+ Slavonic Rhapsody No. 3)

Dvořák overhauled his Second Symphony in 1888 prior to the first performance, but the end movements still might be found overlong and rhetorical.

Supplementary Recordings:

London CS 6524/ CM 9524. London SO/ Kertesz

Decca/Jubilee KJBC 111

Supraphon DV 5539. Prague SO/ Neumann

Artia ALP 141

Opus 9110 0994. Slovak PO/ Košler

MHS 824 824 Y (+ Symphony No. 1) (two LP)

Philips 6500 123. London SO/ Rowicki

SYMPHONY NO. 3 IN E-FLAT MAJOR, op.10 (B.34) (1873)

* Supraphon C37-7668. Czech Philharmonic Orchestra conducted by Václav Neumann

    Supraphon 1110 4135

* Chandos CHAN 8575. Scottish National Orchestra conducted by Neeme Järvi (+ Carnival; Symphonic Variations)

    Chandos ABRD 1270

Unpublished until 1912, the Third is the only Dvořák symphony in three movements. This was one of the works successfully submitted for the Austrian State Prize when Dvořák was a struggling unknown; in turn, this led to lifelong friendshisp with Hanslick and Brahms.

Supplementary Recordings:

    Supraphon 1110 3573. Czech PO/ Neumann (+ Scherzo capriccioso). Rec 1973

    Supraphon SUA ST 50120. Prague SO/ Smetáček

        Artia ALP-136

    Opus 9110 0874. Slovak PO/ Košler

        MHS 824 629 Y (+ Symphony No. 5) (two LP)

    Philips 6500 286. London SO/ Rowicki

    Westminster WN 18067. Vienna SO/ Swoboda (+ Slavonic Rhapsody No. 2; Scherzo capriccioso)

        Westminster WL 5029

    London CS 6525/ CM 9525. London SO/ Kertesz (+ Hussite)

        Decca/Jubilee KJBC 112 (+ Symphonic Variations)

* Virgin Classics VC7 90797-2. Royal Liverpool PO/Pešek (+ Carnival; Scherzo capriccioso)

SYMPHONY NO. 4 IN D MINOR, op.31 (B.41) (1874)

* London 417596-2. London Symphony Orchestra conducted by István Kertész (+ Golden Spinning Wheel)

   London CS 6526/ CM 9526 (+ In Nature's Realm)

   Decca/Jubilee KJBC 113 (+ In Nature's Realm)

* Supraphon C37-7442. Czech Philharmonic Orchestra conducted by Václav Neumann.

* Chandos CHAN 8608. Scottish National Orchestra conducted by Neeme Järvi (+ Biblical Songs)

The Fourth Symphony, rich in distinctive melody, finds Dvořák well along the road to symphonic mastery, even as the ghost of Wagner peeps from many passages. The slow movement (Andante), for instance, seems almost a direct crib from the Pilgrims' Chorus in Tannhäuser.

Supplementary Recordings:

   Supraphon 50119. Prague SO/ Neumann

   Artia ALP-137

   Supraphon 1110 3574. Czech PO/ Neumann. Rec 1973

   Opus 9110 0875. Slovak PO/ Košler

   MHS 824 629 Y (+ Symphony No. 8) (two LP)

   Philips 6500 124. London SO/ Rowicki (+ Othello)

   Grenadilla 1036. New York O Society/ Eger (+ Kodály)

   Concert Hall Society CHS F11. Vienna State Opera O/ Swoboda

SYMPHONY NO. 5 IN F MAJOR, op.76 (B.54) (1875) (Old No.3)

* Supraphon C37-7377. Czech Philharmonic Orchestra conducted by Václav Neumann. Rec 1982

   Supraphon 1110 3407

* London 417 597-2. London Symphony Orchestra conducted by István Kertesz
(+ Hussite; My Home)

    London CS 6511/ CM 9511 (+ My Home)

    Decca/Jubilee KJBC 114 (+ Hussite)

* Chandos CHAN 8552. Scottish National Orchestra conducted by Neeme Järvi
(+ Water Goblin)

    Chandos ARBD 1258

Long known mistakenly as the composer's "Third" Symphony, the F Major still suffers concert hall neglect despite a good supply of recordings. It might stand as Dvořák's pastoral symphony until sudden toughening takes hold in fully elaborated strokes in the final movement (Allergro molto).

Supplementary Recordings:

    CBS IM-37272. Philharmonia O/ Andrew Davis

    Supraphon 1110 3407. Czech PO/Neumann. Rec 1972

    Opus 9110 0660. Slovak PO/ Košler

        MHS 824 629 (+ Symphony No. 3) (two LP)

    Philips 802 820. London SO/Rowicki)+ Carnival)

        World Series PHC 9088

    Classic Excellence CE 11032. Austrian Radio SO/ Swarowsky

    Euphoria E-2057. Bamberg SO/ Swarowsky

    Urania 7153. Leipzig PO/ Schuler

    Supraphon DV 5298. Czech PO/ Šejna

        Artia ALP-171 (+ Othello)

        Rediffusion/Heritage HCN 8016 (+ Smetana)

    Concert Hall Society CHS 1240. Netherlands PO/ Goehr

Meoldya D 03568/9. Moscow Radio O/ Paverman

Supraphon 1110 3654. Karlovy Vary SO/ Eliska (+ In Nature's Realm)

SYMPHONY NO. 6 IN D. MAJOR, op.60 (B.112) (1880) (Old No. 1)

* Supraphon C37-7705. Czech Philharmonic Orchestra conducted by Václav Neumann

* Chandos CHAN 8530. Scottish National Orchestra conducted by Neeme Järvi (+ Noonday Witch)

   Chandos ABRD 1240

* London 417598-2. London Symphony Orchestra conducted by István Kertesz (+ Symphonic Variations)

   London CS 6495 (CM 9495) (+ Carnival)

   Decca/Jubilee KJBC 115 (+ My Home)

* Koss Classics KC 1001. Milwaukee Symphony Orchestra, conducted by Zdenek Macal (+ Hussite)

Design and engineering in Dvořák's D Major Symphony suggest certain parallels to the Brahms Second, but melodic contours and turns of phrase remain true to the Czech master's own idiom. In this one work alone Dvořák can honestly claim title as father of the modern Czech symphony.

Supplementary Recordings:

   Supraphon SUA ST 50746. Czech PO/ Ančerl. Rec 1966

   Crossroads 22 16 0146

   MHS 3559

   Legend 012

* BIS CD 421/414. Stockholm PO/ Ahronovitch. Rec live 1984

   Opus 9110 0588. Slovak PO/ Košler

   MHS 824 332 (+ Symphony No. 7)(two LP)

   CBS IM-36708. Philharmonia O/ Andrew Davis

Supraphon 0 10 1733. Czech PO/ Talich

Columbia ML 4269. Cleveland O/ Leinsdorf

Columbia Special Products P 14159

RCA LSC 3017. Boston SO/ Leinsdorf

Angel SX-37716. London PO/ Rostropovich

HMV/EMI ASD 3169. Royal PO/ Groves

Philips WX 9008. London SO/ Rowicki

World Series PHC 9008

DGG 2530425. Berlin PO/ Kubelik

Supraphon LPV-216. Czech PO/Šejna. Rec 1960

Artia ALP-172

Panton 8110 0389/90. Prague SO/ Smetáček (+ Suk; Mozart) (two LP)

* Virgin Classics VC7 90791-2. Czech PO/ Pešek (+ In Nature's Realm)

SYMPHONY NO. 7 IN D MINOR, op.70 (B.141) (1885) (Old No.2)

* Supraphon C37-7704. Czech Philharmonic Orchestra conducted by Václav Neumann. Rec 1981

    Supraphon 1110 3139

    * ProArte CDS-7067

* Chandos CHAN 8501. Scottish National Orchestra conducted by Neeme Järvi (+ Golden Spinning Wheel)

* London 417-564-2. Cleveland Orchestra conducted by Christoph von Dohnányi

    London 421-081-2 (+ Symphonies 8, 9) (two CD)

* Telarc CD-80173. Los Angeles Philharmonic Orchestra conducted by André Previn (+ My Home)

In the dark-hued Seventh Symphony Dvořák nursed a conscious desire to plant his flag as a major European artist rather than a colorful nationalist from Bohemia. He wanted to create a stir in the world, and the response following the London first performance proved his wish had been granted. The Seventh joined the world repertoire, and connoisseurs have subsequently claimed this his finest example of symphonic writing; to dispute them is difficult. Since the advent of LP records the listener has been offered an embarrassment of riches.

Supplementary Recordings:

Supraphon 50647. Czech PO/ Košler. Rec 1964

Crossroads 22 16 0098

Quintessence PMC 7126

* Supraphonet 11 1106-2 011 (+ Water Goblin)

Opus 9110 0280. Slovak PO/ Košler

MHS 824 332 (+ Symphony No. 6)(two LP)

Angel S-37270. London PO/ Giulini

RCA LM/LSC 2489. London SO/ Monteux

RCA/Victrola 1310

London/STS 15157

Angel SZ-37717. London PO/ Rostropovich

London CS-6607. Israel PO/ Mehta

London CS-2224 (+ Tchaikovsky) (two LP)

Columbia ML 6228. New York PO/ Bernstein

Columbia MS 6828

Supraphon LPV 27. Czech PO/ Šejna

Artia 177 (+ Devil and Kate Ov)

DGG 2530127. Berlin PO/ Kubelik

London LL-1606. Vienna PO/ Kubelik

London/STS 15125

London CS-6402/ CM 9402. London PO/ Kertesz

Decca/Jubilee KJBC 116

Philips 6500 287. London SO/ Rowicki (+ My Home)

RCA ARL1-3555. Philadelphia O/ Ormandy

CBS M 36684. Philharmonia O/ Andrew Davis

CBS M3-36946 (+ Symphonies 8, 9) (three LP)

Columbia MS 7331. Cleveland O/ Szell

CBS Classics 61732

Epic BC 1111

Columbia/Odyssey Y 35931

Columbia D3S 814 (+ Symphonies 8, 9) (three LP)

* DGG 410 997-2. Vienna PO/ Maazel

DGG 410-997-1

* RCA RCD1-5427. Chicago SO/ Levine

RCA ARC1-5427

* Lodia CD 782. The Philharmonia Symphony/ Paita

Lodia LOD 782

* Vox Prima MWCD 7153. London SO/ Mata (+ Elgar)

* Philips 420 890-2. Concertgebouw O/ Colin Davis (+ Symphony No. 8)

* Virgin Classics VC7 90756-2. Royal Liverpool PO/ Pešek (+ Symphony No. 8)

Epic LC 3668. Concertgebouw O/Haitink (+ <u>Slavonic Dances</u> 1, 3, 7, 8)

Spectrum 181. Berlin State Opera O/ Suitner

* EMI CDC 7 49948-2. Philadelphia O/ Sawallisch (+ Symphony No. 8)

SYMPHONY NO. 8 IN G MAJOR, op.88 (B.163)(1889 (Old No.4)

* DGG 415 971-2. Vienna Philharmonic Orchestra conducted by Herbert von Karajan

* Chandos CHAN 8666. Scottish National Orchestra conducted by Neeme Järvi (+ <u>Wood Dove</u>)

    Chandos ABRD 1352

* CBS MK 42038. Columbia Symphony Orchestra conducted by Bruno Walter

    Columbia ML 5761 (MS 6361; MS 6868)

    Columbia/Odyssey YT 33231 (+ Wagner)

* Angel CDC 47618. Cleveland Orchestra conducted by George Szell (+ <u>Slavonic Dances</u> 46/3; 72/2)

* Supraphon C37-7073. Czech Philharmonic Orchestra conducted by Václav Neumann

    Supraphon 1110 3400

    ProArte CDS-7073

The popular but unorthodox G Major Symphony is ingeniously constructed almost entirely around a seamless sequence of melody projected through a prism of telling orchestration. Probably no more Czech-sounding symphony has ever been written. Conductors like Bruno Walter, George Szell and Herbert von Karajan have found this music especially congenial to their talents.

<u>Supplementary Recordings</u>:

    Angel S-60045. Philharmonia O/ Giulini

        Angel/Eminence AE 34449 (+ Symphony No. 9)

        Angel S-35487 (+ <u>Scherzo capriccioso</u>)

* Telarc CD 80206. Los Angeles PO/ Previn (+ <u>Notturno</u>; <u>Scherzo</u> <u>capriccioso</u>)

DGG 2531048. Chicago SO/ Giulini. Rec 1979

London LLP 488. Concertgebouw O/ Szell

   London/STS R-23245

   Turnabout TV-S 34525

Opus 9110 0281. Slovak PO/ Košler

   MHS 827 288 (+ Symphony No. 4) (two LP)

Odeon ALP 2003. Royal PO/ Beecham (+ Wagner)

London CS-6358/ CM-9358. London SO/ Kertész

   Decca/Jubilee KJBC 117

London CS-6443 (CM 9443). Vienna PO/ Karajan. Rec 1964

   * Decca/Ovation 417 744-2DM (+ Brahms)

London/Jubilee KJBC 71 (+ Tchaikovaky)

Angel SZ 37686. Berlin PO/ Karajan (+ <u>Slavonic</u> <u>Dance</u>) 46/8). Rec 1979

Angel 35214. Philharmonia O/ Sawallisch (+ <u>Scherzo</u> <u>capriccioso</u>)

MHS 3400. Yomiuri Nippon SO/ Theodore Guschlbauer

Supraphon 1 10 1203. Czech PO/ Neumann. Rec 1971

   ProArte PAL 1053

   Quintessence PMC 7119

   Vanguard/Supraphon SU-2

Mercury MG 50162. Hallé O/ Barbirolli (+ <u>Scherzo</u> <u>capriccioso</u>)

   Everest 3449

   Mercury SD 162

Philips/Sequenza 6527 199. London SO/ Rowicki

Philips/ Universo 6580 126. Concertgebouw O/ Haitink (+ <u>Slavonic Dances</u> 46/2, 4, 6)

RCA ARL1-4264. Philadelphia O/ Ormandy

* Supraphon/ Treasury DC 8051. Czech PO/ Neumann (+ <u>In Nature Realm</u>; Smetana)

* Lodia CO-CD 789. Royal PO/ Paita (+ Symphony No. 9)

CBS/Masterworks M-35865. Philharmonia O/ Andrew Davis (+ <u>Carnival</u>)

Panton 01 447/8. Czech PO/ Stupka (+ Symphony No.9)(two LP)

Supraphon DV 5057. Czech PO/ Talich

    Supraphon LPV 44

    Artia ALP-178 (+ <u>Midday Witch</u>)

Angel SZ-37719. Los Angeles PO/ Mehta (+ <u>Wood Dove</u>)

HMV 1014. Philharmonia O/ Kubelik

    RCA LHMV 1014

Remington 199-168. Cincinnati SO/ Johnson. Rec 1953

    Varese-Sarabande V 81044

Nonesuch H 71262. Hamburg PO/ Mackerras

    Checkmate C-76006

Vox PL-11050. Bamberg SO/ Perlea

    Vox STPL 511050

Angel 35622. London PO/ Silvestri (+ <u>Carnival</u>)

    Classics for Pleasure CPF 40075

Balkaton BCA 10364. Sofia SO/ Iliev

CBS/Great Performances MYK 38470. Cleveland O/ Szell. Rec 1958

Epic LC 3532

CBS MY 38470

Columbia D3S-814 (+ Symphonies 7, 9) (three LP)

Mercury 50236. London SO/ Dorati (+ <u>Carnival</u>)

Mercury 18080

RCA DRL1-0051. Boston SO/ Munch

RCA LM/LSC 2629

RCA ARL1-3550. Sydney SO/ Serebrier

* Virgin Classics VC7 90756-2. Royal Liverpool PO/ Pešek
  (+ Symphony No. 7)

* EMI CDC 7 49948-2. Philadelphia O/ Sawallisch (+ Symphony No. 7)

* Academy Sound and Vision CD QS 6006. Royal Liverpool PO/ Batiz
  (+ <u>Carnival</u>). Rec 1986

  Academy Sound and Vision ALH/ZCALH 912 (2856). Hallé O/ Loughran
  (+ <u>Carnival</u>)

* Philips 412542-2. Minnesota O/ Marriner (+ Symphonies 7, 9) (two CD)

  Philips 412 542-1

  DGG 139 181. Berlin PO/ Kubelik

  DGG/Privilege 2535 397-10

* Perpetua PR 7007. Philharmonia Hungarica/ McRae

  Urania URLP 7160. Leipzig PO/ Pfluger

* Stradivari SCD 5056. Ljubljana SO/ Nanut (+ Smetana)

  DGG 18141. Bamberg SO/ Lehmann

* Chandos CD 8323. London PO/ Handley (+ <u>Notturno</u>)

  Chandos ABRD 1105

* DGG 415205-2. Vienna PO/ Maazel

  DGG 3302 034

* Spectrum SR-181. Berlin SO/ Suitner (+ <u>Carnival</u>)

* Centaur CRC 2018. Houston SO/ Comissiona. Rec 1984

* London 414 222-2. Cleveland O/ Dohnányi (+ <u>Scherzo capriccioso</u>)

  London 414 422-1

* Philips 420 890-2. Concertgebouw O/ Colin Davis (+ Symphony No. 7)

* Philips CD 420 399-2 (+ <u>Symphonic Variations</u>)

  Philips 9500 317

* Deutsche Schallplatten 32TC-41. Staatskapelle Dresden/ Blomstedt

* Compact Classics CD 516. London SO/ Ludwig (+ Symphony No. 9)

* Koss Classics KC 1002. Milwaukee SO/ Macal (+ <u>Czech Suite</u>)

* AS Disc AS 411. New York PO/Bruno Walter (+ Chopin). Rec 1948

SYMPHONY NO. 9 IN E MINOR, op.95 (B.178). "FROM THE WORLD"
(Z NOVÉHO SVĚTA) (1893) (Old No.5)

* RCA RCCD-1008. NBC Symphony Orchestra conducted by Arturo Toscanini
  (+ Smetana)

  RCA LM-1778

  RCA/Victrola-1249 (+ Schumann)

  RCA LME-2408

* RCA 5606-2-RC. Chicago Symphony Orchestra conducted by Fritz Reiner
  (+ <u>Carnival</u>; Smetana; Weinberger)

  RCA LM/LSC 2214

* London 400047-2.   Vienna Philharmonic Orchestra conducted by Kiril Kondrashin

   London LDR 10011

   London/Jubilee 417-267 (+ Slavonic Dances selections)

* London 414421-2. Cleveland Orchestra conducted by Christoph von Dohnanyi

   London 414421-1

   * 2-London 421082-2 (+ Symphonies 7,8) (two CD)

   DGG 415915-1. Berlin Philharmonic Orchestra conducted by Raphael Kubelik

   DGG 2530 415

   DGG/Signature 2543 513

Audience loyalty towards the Ninth Symphony has shown no sign of receding since applause rocked Carnegie Hall at the premiere 16 December 1893. After almost one hundred years the "New World" remains among the most often-performed (and recorded) symphonies of all time. How much, if any, actual American Indian and Negro material shaped these forceful themes and vibrant rhythms has led to much mulling over sketchbooks and the composer's sometimes enigmatic statements. But his cannily-constructed opus probably could never have achieved its present state without Dvořák's residence in the United States, and his sensitive absorption of what he honestly believed to be genuine Americana.

Supplementary Recordings:

RECORDINGS OF CZECHOSLOVAK ORIGIN:

* Supraphon C37-7702. Czech PO/ Neumann. Rec 1982

   Supraphon 1110 3140

   ProArte PDD 157

* Pierre Verany PV 087011. Slovak PO/ Redel (+ Smetana)

* Enigma Classics 7 74600-2. CSR Symphony Orchestra (Bratislava)/ Lenárd (+ Slavonic Dances selections)

* LaserLight 15517. Prague Festival O/ Urbanek (+ Romance, op.11; Carnival)

* Sonata CD 91018. Slovak PO/ Pešek

* Opus 9150 0282. Slovak PO/ Košler. Rec 1973

Opus 9110 0282

MHS 4084

Supraphon 50433 (10 8061-1 211) Czech PO/ Ančerl

Supraphon DV 5859

Parliament PLP-170

Rediffusion/Legend LGD 004

Supraphon 10128. Czech PO. Talich

Artia ALP 190

Parliament PLP 101

Supraphon DV 5237

Colosseum 162/3 (+ <u>Stabat</u> <u>Mater</u>) (two LP)

* Supraphon 11 0290-2 001 (+ Serenade for Strings)

Panton 01 0447/8. Czech PO/ Stupka (+ Symphony No. 8)

* Supraphon/Gems 2SUP-0003.   Czech PO/ Neumann (+ <u>Symphonic</u> <u>Variations)</u>. Rec 1972

* Supraphon DC 8031 (+ <u>Carnival</u>; Smetana)

Supraphon 1 10 1334

Vanguard/Supraphon SV 8

Fortuna TLPS 967. Prague SO/ Marek

RECORDINGS OF AUSTRO-GERMAN ORIGIN:

* Angel CDC-47071-2. Berlin PO/ Tennstedt

   Angel DS-38140

* DGG 410 032-2. Vienna PO/ Maazel (+ <u>Carnival</u>)

   DGG 253 2079 (+ <u>Carnival</u>)

* DGG 415509-2. Vienna PO/ Karajan (+ Smetana)

   DGG 415509-1

* Teldec 8.43 359 ZK. Bamberg SO/ Keilberth (+ <u>Carnival</u>)

   Teldec/Aspekte 6.43319

* Concerto Collection INT 820.716. Rheinische Philharmonie Koblenz/ Crabeels (+ <u>Serenade</u>, op.22)

* DGG Mono 423 528-2. Berlin PO/ Karajan (+ J. Strauss) in Karajan: The First Recordings. Rec 1940

* DGG 423 206-2. Berlin PO/ Karajan (+ <u>Slavonic Dances</u> selections). Rec 1964

   DGG 138 922

   Angel S-37437. Berlin PO/ Karajan (+ Smetana). Rec 1977

   * Angel/ Studio Series 769005-2 (+ Smetana)

   DGG 138127. RIAS SO/ Fricsay

   DGG/Privilege/Resonance 2535 141

* DGG 423384-2. Berlin PO/ Fricsay (+ Liszt; Smetana)

   Summit SUM 5036. Radio SO Salzburg/ Moralt

* Allegro II ACD 8008. Bamberg SO/ Hollreiser. Rec 1959

   Vox STPL 510.810

* Conifer Compact Disc Selection TQ 126. South German Philharmonic Stuttgart/ Alolph (+ Smetana)

* AS Disc AS-111. Berlin PO/ Furtwängler; NBC SO/ Toscanini. Rec 1941, 1953

    Relief 813 (Furtwängler) (May be spurious. See page xviii)

* London/Weekend 417 678-2. Vienna PO/ Kertesz (+ Smetana)

    London CS-6228 (STS 15101)

London CS-6020. Vienna PO/ Kubelik. Rec 1955

    London LL-1607 (STS 15007)

DGG 2531 098. Vienna PO/ Bohm

    DGG/Galleria 415 837-1 (+ Symphonic Variations)

Vox PL 7590. Vienna State Philharmonia/ Horenstein

Bruno Walter Society. Berlin State Opera O/ Erich Kleiber
(+ Mozart)

Longanesi Periodici/ I Grandi Concerti 8. WDR SO Cologne/ Erich Kleiber

Arabesque 8019. Berlin PO/ Kempe (+ Scherzo capriccioso)

Philips PHS 900-161. Radio SO Berlin/ Maazel

    Philips Festivo 6570 169 (+ Smetana)

Vanguard Stereo Lab SRV-114. Vienna State Opera O/ Golschmann

    Vanguard/Everyman SRV 208 SD

Erato STU 70444. Northwest German P/ Lindberg

Urania 7132. Radio Leipzig SO/ Pflüger (+ Smetana)

Whitehall WH 40015. Vienna Festival O/ Vernal

Emidisc C 047-50 508. Berlin PO/Kempe

RECORDINGS OF AMERICAN ORIGIN:

* RCA/Papillon Collection 6530-2 RG. Boston SO/ Fiedler (+ <u>Carnival</u>; <u>Humoresque-Swanee River</u>; Enesco)

    RCA LSC 3134

    RCA/Gold Seal AGL1-3364 (AGL1-5204)

* RCA RCD1-4552. Chicago SO/ Levine. Rec 1981

    RCA ARC1-4552

* CBS MYK-37763. Cleveland O/ Szell

    Columbia ML 4541

    CBS MY-37763

* CBS MK 42417. Cleveland O/ Szell (+ <u>Carnival</u>; <u>Slavonic Dances</u> 46/1,8; Smetana) Rec 1959

* CBS MK-42039. Columbia SO/ Walter. Rec 1960

    Columbia ML-5384

    Columbia/Odyssey Y 30045

    Columbia MS-6066

    Columbia MS-6393. New York PO/ Bernstein

    Columbia ML-5793

    Columbia M 31809

    Mercury MG 50002. Chicago SO/ Kubelik

    Wing 14021

    Telarc Digital DG-10053. St. Louis SO/ Slatkin

Angel AM-34700. Philadelphia O/ Muti

Angel S-37230

* Angel CDC 49114. Philadelphia O/ Sawallisch (+ Scherzo capriccioso)

RCA ARL1-2949. Philadelphia O/ Ormandy

Columbia ML-5115. Philadelphia O/ Ormandy

Columbia ML-4023. Philadelphia O/ Ormandy

Columbia CL-731

* Philips 412541-2. Minnesota O/ Marriner (+ Symphonies 7, 8) (two CD). Rec 1984

Philips 412-224-1

* DGG/Galleria 423882-2. Chicago SO/ Giulini (+ Schubert)

DGG 2530 881

* Hunt Productions CD 34017. NBC SO/ Toscanini (+ Symphonic Variations). Rec live 1953 (Symphony No. 9); 1951 (Symphonic Variations)

   * Nuova Era 013.6311/12 (+ Mendelssohn et al) (two CD)

   * AS Disc AS 111 (+ Symphony No. 9 cond Furtwängler)

   * Virtuoso 269 7012 (+ Mussorgsky)

* Nuova Era 2297. New York PO/ de Sabata (+ Barber)

RCA CRL2-0334. Philadelphia O; New Philharmonia O/ Stokowski. Rec 1927 (Philadelphia); 1973 (New Philharmonia)

RCA LM 1013. Stokowski and his Symphony O

RCA/Camden CAL-104 (CDN-1008). Philadelphia O/ Stokowski. Note: some issues list "Warwick Symphony Orchestra."

Philips 9500001. San Francisco SO/ Ozawa. Rec 1975

   * Philips/ Concert Classics 426 073-2 (+ Carnival)

Capitol SP 8454. Los Angeles PO/ Leinsdorf

Pickwick PC/SPC 4005

London CS 6980. Los Angeles PO/ Mehta (+ Carnival)

' Mercury 50262 (90262). Detroit SO/ Paray

World Record Club T 10. Symphony of the Air (without conductor)

Oryx BRL 94. SO of Philadelphia Music Guild/ Masters

Music Appreciation Records MAR 6237. Stadium Concerts SO/ Bernstein (with analysis by Leonard Bernstein on accompanying ten-inch disc)

Lyrique HPG 1019. Cincinnati ProArte O/ Duhamel

RECORDINGS OF BRITISH ORIGIN:

* Angel/ Laser Series CDZ 7 62514 2. Philharmonia O/ Giulini (+ Carnival; Scherzo capriccioso)

  Angel/Eminence AE 34449 (+ Symphony No. 8)

  Seraphim S-60045 (+ Carnival)

* Varèse-Sarabande VCD-47216. London PO/ Batiz (+ Carnival)

  Varese-Sarabande 704190

* Angel CDB 62006. London PO/ Macal (+ Symphonic Varations)

  Classics for Pleasure CFP 104

* MCA Classics MCAD-25961. London SO/ Tuckwell (+ Carnival)

  MCA-25961

* Bescol CD 516. London SO/ Ludwig (+ Symphony No. 8)

  Everest S-3056

* Virgin Classics VC 7 90723-2. Royal Liverpool SO/ Pešek (+ American Suite)

* MHS 512245 W. London PO/ Macal

  MHS 512245F

* London/Jubilee 417724-2. London SO/ Kertesz (+ Carnival; Scherzo capriciosso)

  London CM 9527/ CS 6527 (+ Othello)

* Collins Classics 1002-2. London PO/ Loughran

* CALA TT 72.22. London SO/ Simon (+ Grieg; Josephs)

* Nieman-Marcus/Vox NMCD-1. London SO/ Simon (+ Grieg; Josephs)

  Angel SZ-37119. London PO/ Rostropovich. Rec 1979

  Angel S-37230. New Philharmonia O/ Muti

  Angel 35085. Philharmonia O/ Galliera

  Angel 36246. Philharmonia O/ Klemperer

    Angel/Redline RL 32003

* Menuet 160014-2. Royal PO/ Kempe (+ R. Strauss)

  Westminster 18295. Philharmonic Symphony of London/ Rodzinski

    Westminster WL 5370

    Music Guild IDS-9903

  London LLP 432. New SO/ Jorda

    Richmond B-19003

  Philips 802903. London SO/ Rowicki

    Philips/Sequenza 6527-192

  Audio Award AA-216. London PO/ Handley

  PYE GSGC 14070. Halle O/ Barbirolli

    Vanguard/Everyman SRV 182 SD

Alshire SSC-10019. London PO/ Rignold

   Somerset SF-13100

   Audio Spectrum ASC-10019

Columbia Musical Treasures DMS-396. London PO/ Gibson

Capitol P-8308. New SO/ Rudolph Schwarz

CBS M3-36946. Philharmonia O/ Andrew Davis (+ Symphonies 7, 8)

   CBS-M-35834

Columbia MS-7089. London SO/ Ormandy

Turnabout 34702. Royal PO/ /Dorati

London SPC 21025. New Philharmonia O/ Dorati

   London/STS 15567

Classics for Pleasure CFP 104. Philharmonia O/ Sawallisch
(+ Carnival)

* Chandos CHAN 8510. Scottish National O/ Järvi (+ My Home)

   Chandos ABRD 1220

* Compact Classics CD 516. London SO/ Ludwig (+ Symphony No. 8)

   Everest 6056 (3056)

   Vanguard/Everyman SRV-182. Halle' O/ Barbirolli

* Chesky Records CD 31. Royal PO/ Horenstein (+ Wagner)

   Quintessence 7001

RECORDINGS FROM DIVERSE SOURCES:

* Erato/Success ECD 40005. Orchestre Philharmonie de Strasbourg/ Lombard

   Erato STU 71085

* Black Pearl BPCD 2019. Radio Luxembourg SO/ Froment

* Teldec 243-731-2. Concertgebouw O/ Mengelberg. Rec 1941

* White Label HRC 064. Hungarian State O/ Patané (+ Smetana)

    Hungaroton SLPD 12501

* Philips/ Silver Line 420349-2. Concertgebouw O/ Colin Davis (+ <u>Symphonic Variations</u>)

    Philips 412921-1

    Philips 6998 029 (+ Symphonies 7, 8) (three LP)

* Price-Less D 16530. Zurich Tonhalle O/ Josef Krips. Rec 1960

    Festival Classique FC-409

* Stradivari SCD-6030. Slovenian PO/ Horvat (+ <u>Carnival</u>; Glinka) Rec 1987

* Hunt Productions CD 526. Turin SO of the RAI/ Celibidache (+ Borodin; Bartok)

RCA/Bluebird WBC/LBC 1005. Danish National O/ Malko

Allegro 1671. Oslo PO/ Grüner-Hegge

MHS DRM 112. Philharmonia Hungarica/ Albert. Rec 1979

    Oryx EXP 45

Egmont EGM 7023. Budapest O/ Valescu

Musical Masterpiece Society MMS 36. Zurich Tonhalle O/ Ackermann (ten-inch LP)

Epic 3001. Hague PO/ Dorati

    Philips A 00154

Eurodisc 28 342 KK. USSR Large SO/ Rozhdestvensky. Rec 1973

Lyrinx LYR 063. L'orchestre des Jeunes de la Mediteranée en concert/ Tabachnik

Melodya C-0397/98. State SO/ Anosov

Camerata CMT 1003. Tokyo PO/ Otaka

Connoisseur 2108. O of Paris/ Prêtre

Angel 35623. Radiodiffusion Français O/ Silvestri

Peerless EXP 45. Hungarian PO/ Albert

Tudor 73002. Tonhalle O Zurich/ Kempe

* AS Disc AS-312. Danish Radio SO/ Busch in "Fritz Busch Edition" Vol II. Rec 1933 (+ Carnival)

* Angel 49860-2. Oslo PO/Janssons (+ Smetana)

* London 421 016. Concertgebouw O/Chailly (+ Carnival)

* Digital Concerto CCT 611. Ljubljana Radio SO/ Nanut (+ Slavonic Dances 72/l, 2; Smetana)

* DGG 427 346-2. Israel PO/ Bernstein (+ Slavonic Dances Nos. l, 3, 8)

DGG 427 346-1

Additional Recordings:

Rondo ST 569 (Berlin SO/ Weth); CMS Summit 1013 (Pro Musica S/ Walther); Masterseal MSLP 5014 (Viennese SO/ Singer); Remington RLP-199-4 (Vienna Symphony Society/ Woss); Contour 2870 118 (Berlin PO/ Gerdes); Crown Records CLP-5137 (Hamburg PO/Jergens); Grand Awards GA 224 (Hamburg Pro Musica/ Walther); Remington 3/ Concerteum CR 245 (Austrian SO/ Singer); Telefunken LGX 66007 (NWDR SO/ Schmidt-Isserstedt); Classica CLA 102 (Frankfurt SO/ Langer); American Home Library 6002 (Hamburg International PO/ von Luden); Royale 123 (Berlin SO/List); Plymouth P 12-14 (Vienna Tonkunstler O/?); Cwaliton QLP-1000 (Welsh National Youth S/ Raybold); Design DLP 124 (Hampshire PO/ Halloway): Promenade 2104 (Sonar SO/Lederman); Sine Qua Non/Masterpiece Series 74007 (Bamberg

SO/Swarowsky) in "Romantic Symphonies"; Bell LP 30 (Hamburg SO/Otto Schmidt).

Overtures, Rhapsodies and Tone Poems:

TRAGIC (DRAMATIC) OVERTURE, (b.16a) (1870)

See the opera Alfred, overture.

CONCERT OVERTURE IN F MAJOR (B.21a) (1871)

Another name for the overture to the first version of King and Charcoal Burner; Marco Polo 8.223272 in "Dvořák Opera Overtures and Preludes."

SYMPHONIC POEM (RHAPSODY) IN A MINOR, op.14 (B.44) (1874)

* Records International 7013-2. Slovak Philharmonic Orchestra conducted by Libor Pešek (+ Vanda; Cunning Peasant; Dramatic overtures). Rec 1986

* Marco Polo 622 420 TZ

SLAVONIC RHAPSODIES: NO. 1 IN D; NO. 2 IN G MINOR; NO. 3 IN A-FLAT MAJOR, op.45 (B.86) (1878)

* Philips 416 623-2 and 416 624-2. Leipzig Gewandhaus Orchestra conducted by Kurt Masur (+ Slavonic Dances) (two CD)

Supraphon 1 10 1459. Czech Philharmonic Orchestra conducted by Václav Neumann (+ Wood Dove)

Telefunken 6.35075. Czech Philharmonic Orchestra conducte by Václav Neumann (+ Slavonic Dances; Czech Suite; Wood Dove) (three LP)

Telefunken 6.42203 (+ Slavonic Dances, op.46)

The three Slavonic Rhapsodies (sometimes confused with the more popular Slavonic Dances) are symphonic movements invoking memories of distant Slavdom. These are rough equivalents to the tone poems constituting Smetana's cycle Ma Vlast. Each manifests ample bardic color, but No. 3 seems the most coherent and tuneful.

Supplemental Recordings:

Slavonic Rhapsodies Nos. 1-3:

>Supraphon LPV 407 (DV 5495). Cezch PO/ Šejna (+ Scherzo capriccioso)

Slavonic Rhapsody No. 1:

* * Teldec 8.42203. Czech PO/Neumann (+ Slavonic Dances)

* * Marco Polo 8.223129. Slovak PO/Košler (+ Rhapsody No. 3; Slavonic Dances)

> Epic SC-60626. Concertgebouw O/Dorati (+ Rhapsody No. 2; Smetana) (two LP)

> Supraphon LPM 198. Czech PO/Šejna (+ Rhapsody No. 2) (ten-inch LP)

Slavonic Rhapsody No. 2:

* * Teldec 8.44072. Czech PO/Neumann (+ Rhapsody No. 3; Slavonic Dances)

> Westminster XWN 19072. Vienna State Opera O/Somogyi (+ Nature, Love, Life). Rec 1964

>> Westminster Gold WGS 8298

> Westminster WL 5008. Vienna SO/ Swoboda (+ Rimsky-Korsakov)

>> Westminster WN 18067 (Symphony No. 3; Scherzo capriccioso)

> Decca (USA) 9850. Bamberg SO/Lehmann (+ Rhapody No. 3; Seranade, op. 22)

> Epic SC 6026. Concertgebouw O/Dorati (+ Rhapsody No. 1; Smetana) (two LP)

> Supraphon LM 198. Czech PO/Šejna (+ Rhapsody No. 1) (ten-inch LP)

Slavonic Rhapsody No.3:

* Chandos CHAN-8589. Scottish National O/ Järvi (+ Symphony No. 2)

* Teldec 8.44072. Czech PO/Neumann (+ Rhapsody No. 2; Slavonic Dances, op.46)

  London CS 7119. Detroit SO/ Dorati (Enesco; Liszt; Ravel)

  EMI SLS 5151. Staatskapelle Dresden/ Berglund (+ Scherzo capriccioso; Smetana) (two LP)

  Angel S-3870 (two LP)

  Capitol G-7107. Royal PO/ Kubelik (+ Scherzo capriccioso; Brahms)

  Decca (USA) DL-4016. Bamberg SO/ Lehmann (+ Rhapsody No. 2) (ten-inch LP)

  Supraphon LPM-203. Czech PO/ Šejna (+ Hussite)(ten-inch LP)

  Epic 3015. Hague PO Residentie/ Dorati (+ Smetana; Mussorgsky)

  Classics for Pleasure 40314. London PO/ Davison (+ Symphony No. 7)

  Melodya D 03064/5. USSR SO/ Khaikin

  Panton 01 0619-21. Prague Radio O/Klima (+ Slavonic Dances)

MY HOME (DOMOV MUJ), op.62 (B.125a) (1882)

* Teldec CD 80173. Los Angeles Philharmonic Orchestra conducted by André Previn (+ Symphony No. 7)

* Chandos CHAN 8510. Scottish National Orchestra conducted by Neeme Järvi (+ Symphony No. 9)

* London 417 597-2. London Symphony Orchestra conducted by István Kertész (+ Hussite; Symphony No. 5)

  London 6746 (+ Hussite; Water Goblin)

  London CS 6511/ CM 9511 (+ Symphony No. 5)

The speedily-written, forceful My Home is an openly patriotic gesture originating in incidental music to a play about the dramatist Josef Kajetan Tyl (1808-1856); he incidentally penned the words to what became the Czech natonal anthem "Where is my home?" Dvořák freely built his overture around the companion tune and a native folk song.

Supplementary Recordings:

  Supraphon 1110 2968. Czech PO/ Neumann (Overtures)

  Panton 8110 0106. Kromeříž Conservatory O/ Hyl (Myslivecek; Gregor; Harasta)

  Supraphon 4 10 1990. Prague Radio SO/ Krombholc (Overtures)

    Supraphon/ Gemini 1 SUPD 006 (+ Overtures; Song Cycles) (two LP)

  DGG 2530593. Bavarian Radio SO/ Kubelik (+ Slavonic Dances, op.72)

  Supraphon 50432. Czech PO/ Ančerl (+ Overtures)

* Supraphon/ Crystal 11 0605 2011 (+ Overtures)

  Classics for Pleasure CFP 145

  Supraphon 1 10 1589. (+ Nature's Realm; Smetana)

  Philips 6500 287. London SO/Rowicki (+ Symphony No. 7)

HUSSITE OVERTURE (HUSITSKÁ), op,67 (B.132) (1883)

* London 414 597-2. London Symphony Orchestra conducted by István Kertész (+ My Home; Symphony No. 5)

  London 6746 (+ My Home; Water Goblin)

  London CS 6525/ CM 9525 (+ Symphony No. 3)

* Supraphon/Gems 2 SUP-0028. Czech Philharmonic Orchestra conducted by Václav Neumann (+ three tone poems)

Supraphon 4 10 2591/2 (+ four tone poems) (two LP)

Like all Czechs, Dvorak viewed the martyred religious reformer Jan Hus (1374-1415) as a national hero. He entertained no inhibitions about letting hs dramatic overture go full throttle to assertively recapture the turbulent Hussite experience with quotations from their battle songs like "Ye warriors of God" and the "St. Wenceslas Chorale." If not Dvorak's most subtle opus, this rousing overture synopsizes the national sentiment loudly, but with full clarity and conviction.

Supplementary Recordings:

Supraphon 50455. Czech PO/ Ančerl (+ two tone poems)

* Supraphon/ Crystal 11 0605 2011 (+ Overtures)

Supraphon LPM 203. Czech PO/ Šejna (+ Rhapsody No.3) (ten-inch LP)

RCA LM-9017. Boston Pops O/ Fiedler (+ Smetana; Brahms)

RCA LM-1 (+ Smetana) (ten-inch LP)

DGG 2530785. Bavarian Radio SO/ Kubelik (+ Nature's Realm; Carnival)

Philips 6770 045. London SO/ Rowicki (+ Symphonies 1-9)

American Record Society/ Perspectives in Music 34. Performers not stated (+ Haydn; Rossini)

* Koss Classics KC 1001. Milwaukee SO/ Macal (+ Symphony No. 6)

OVERTURE CYCLE: NATURE, LIFE AND LOVE

I: IN NATURE'S REALM (V PŘÍRODÉ), op.91 (B.168) (1891)

II: CARNIVAL, op.92 (B.169) (1891)

III: OTHELLO, op.93 (B.174) (1892)

* Chandos CHAN 6453. Ulster Orchestra conducted by Vernon Handley (+ Scherzo capriccioso). Rec 1985

Chandos ABRD 1163

Supraphon 1110 2968. Czech Phiharmonic Orchestra conducted by Václav Neumann (+ My Home)

ProArte PAL-1054

DGG 2530785. Bavarian Radio Symphony Orchestra conducted by Raphael Kubelik (+ Hussite)

Central to Dvořák's symphonic thought is this tryptich of overtures collectively designated "Nature, Life and Love." Performances as a unit remain rare, while the entities reach recordings piecemeal more often than not. These quasi-programmatic overtures contain thematic cross-references representing the benign and evil forces of nature: In Nature's Realm paints a pantheistic sundown scene when the inner voices of nature resonate in the soul; Carnival (soaring above the others in popularity) charges after zestful living; Othello masterfully distills the poisonous tragedy entrapping the Moor of Venice and his guiltless Desdemona, the dark underside of nature. The set belongs to Dvořák's finest and most rewarding attainments as an orchestral master.

Supplemental Recordings:

Complete Cycle

* Supraphon/Crystal 11 605 2011. Czech PO/ Ančerl (+ My Home; Hussite)

  Supraphon 50432 (+ My Home)

  Supraphon 410 1990. Prague Radio SO/ Krombholc (+ My Home)

  Supraphon/Gemini 1 SUPD 006 (+ My Home; Song cycles) (two LP)

  Westminster 8298. Vienna State Opera O/ Somogyi (+ Slavonic Rhapsody No. 2)

  London 6574. London SO/ Kertesz (+ Scherzo capriccioso)

  Concert Hall Society 1141. Vienna State Opera O/ Swoboda (+ Notturno)

In Nature's Realm:

* Virgin Classics VC7 90791-2. Czech PO/ Pešek (+ Symphony No. 6)

* Supraphon/ Treasury DC 8051. Czech PO/ Neumann (+ Symphony No. 8)

* Philips 420607-2. Concertgebouw O/ Dorati (+ Smetana) (two CD)

  London CM 9526 (CS 6526). London SO/ Kertesz (+ Symphony No. 4)

Supraphon 1110 3654. Karlovy Vary SO/ Eliska (+ Symphony No. 5)

Supraphon 1 10 1589. Czech PO/ Ančerl (+ <u>My Home</u>; Smetana)

<u>Carnival</u> (Karneval; Carnaval):

* RCA 5606-2. Chicago SO/ Reiner (+ Symphony No. 9; Smetana; Weinberger)

    RCA LM 1999

* CBS MYK-36716. Cleveland O/ Szell (+ <u>Slavonic Dances</u>; Smetana)

    * CBS MK-42417 (+ Symphony No.9; <u>Slavonic Dances</u>; Smetanta)

* DGG 410032-2. Vienna PO/ Maazel (+ Symphony No. 9)

* Chandos CHAN 8575. Scottish National O/ Järvi (+ Symphony No. 3); <u>Symphonic Variations</u>)

* Chandos CHAN 8767. Ulster O/ Handley (+ Tchaikovsky et al) in "Romantic Favorites"

    RCA/Victrola 1442. Slovak PO/ Slovak (+ Smetana et al)

    Opus 9110 0454. Slovak PO/ Rajter (+ Svendsen et al)

* Stradivari Classics SCD-6300. Lubljana Radio SO/ Nanut (+ Suppe et al)

    CBS MS-6879. New York PO/ Bernstein (+ <u>Slavonic Dances</u>; Smetana)

    Columbia M 31817

    Columbia ML-5242. Philadelphia O/ Ormandy (+ Enesco; Tchaikovsky)

    RCA AGL1 3967. Boston SO/ Fiedler (+ Dukas et al)

    DGG/ Privilege 2532 234. Berlin Radio SO/ Paul Strauss (+ Smetana et al)

    London STS 15547. London SO/ Kertesz (+ Suppe et al)

    Quintessence 2711. Czech PO/ Ančerl (+ Cello Concerto; Violin Concerto; <u>Romance</u>) (two LP)

    Supraphon DV 5857; SV 3084 (+ <u>In Nature</u>; <u>Othello</u>; <u>My Home</u>)

Saga XID 5028. Royal Danish O/ Frandsen (+ Brahms et al)
* MCA MCAD 25961. London SO/ Tuckwell (+ Symphony No. 9)

Othello:

London CM 9427 (CS 6527). London SO/ Kertesz (+ Symphony No. 9)

Vox Box SVBX 3159 (+ Symphonies 7, 8, 9; Scherzo capriccioso)

Supraphon DM 5018. Czech PO/ Talich (+ Midday Witch)

Artia ALP-171 (+ Symphony No. 5)

Four Erben Tone Poems:

THE WATER GOBLIN (Vodník), op.107 (B.195) (1896)

THE MIDDAY WITCH (Noonday Witch; Polednica), op.108 (B.196) (1896)

THE GOLDEN SPINNING WHEEL (Zlatý kolovrat), op.109 (B.197) (1896)

THE WOOD DOVE (Wild Dove; Holoubek), op.110 (B.197) (1896)

Complete Sets

Supraphon 4 10 2591/92. Czech Philharmonic Orchestra conducted by Václav Neumann (+ Hussite) (two LP)

* Chandos CHAN 8798/99. Scottish National Orchestra conducted by Neeme Järvi (+ Heroic Song; My Home) (two CD)

* Supraphon CO-2196/97. Czech Philharmonic Orchestra conducted by Bohumil Gregor (+ Heroic Song) (two CD)

* Opus 9150 19967/68. Slovak Philharmonic Orchestra conducted by Zdeněk Košler (+ Heroic Song) (two CD)

Opus 9110 1431/33 (+ Symphonic Variations) (three LP)

MHS 930711 W (three LP)

* Supraphon/ Gems 2 SUP 0028. Czech Philharmonic Orchestra conducted by Václav Neumann; Midday Witch; WaterGoblin; Wood Dove (+ Hussite)

* Supraphon/ Gems 2 SUP-0009. Czech Philharmonic Orchestra conducted by Václav Neumann: The Golden Spinning Wheel (+ Cello Concerto No. l; Polonaise)

* Supraphon DC-08056. Czech Philharmonic Orchestra conducted by Václav Neumann: Water Goblin; Midday Witch; Golden Spinning Wheel

* Chandos CHAN 8552. Scottish National Orchestra conducted by Neeme Järvi; Water Goblin (+ Symphony No. 5)

    Chandos ABRD 1258

* Chandos CHAN 8530. Scottish National Orchestra conducted by Neeme Järvi: Midday Witch (+ Symphony No. 6)

    Chandos ABRD 1240

* Chandos 8501. Scottish National Orchestra conducted by Neeme Järvi: Golden Spinning Wheel (+ Symphony No. 7)

    Chandos ABRD 1211

* Chandos CHAN 8666. Scottish National Orchestra conducted by Neeme Järvi: Wood Dove (+ Symphony No. 8)

    Chandos ABRD 1352

Recent years have seen growing appreciation for Dvořák's final statements in symphonic dress expand into multiple recordings, the four tone poems based on the grisly folk ballads of Karel Jaromir Erben (1811-1870) in particular. These gnarly tales have a German counterpart in Des Knaben Wunderhorn which so fascinated Gustav Mahler. Dvořák keeps his symphonic flow close to the poet's lines with meticulous attention to the metrical pattern. Although this literalness finds musical realization in the rondo principle, the listener is advised to be familiar with Erben's texts which can mean the difference between comprehension and puzzlement. As routed through Dvořák, Erben's terror tales for children receive a bounty of inspired melody cloaked in gorgeous orchestration. But The Golden Spinning Wheel seems to crown the set in terms of spell-binding music.

Supplementary Recordings:

* Big Ben 571 010-2. Malmo SO/ Handley: Wood Dove; Golden Spinning Wheel; Water Goblin

* Urania US-5172-CD. Czech PO/ Chalabala. Midday Witch; Wild Dove; Golden Spinning Wheel (from Supraphon 50435)

* Urania US-5161-CD. Czech PO/ Chalabala: Water Goblin (+ Hussite; Specter's Bride; Smetana) (from Supraphon 50455)

    EMI/ Retrospect SH 1003. Royal PO/ Beecham: Golden Spinning Wheel (+ Massenet et al)

* London 417 596-2. London SO/ Kertesz: <u>Golden Spinning Wheel</u> (+ Symphony No. 4)

    Decca/ Jubilee (+ <u>Carnival</u>; <u>Scherzo capriccioso</u>)

    London CS 6721 (+ <u>Symphonic Variations</u>)

London 6746. London SO/ Kertesz: <u>Midday Witch</u>; <u>Water Goblin</u> (+ <u>Hussite</u>; <u>My Home</u>)

DGG 2530 712. Bavarian Radio SO/ Kubelik: <u>Water Goblin</u>; <u>Midday Witch</u> (+ <u>Symphonic Variations</u>)

DGG 2530 713. Bavarian Radio SO/ Kubelik: <u>Wood Dove</u>; <u>Golden Spinning Wheel</u>

Supraphon DV 5002 (LPV-6). Czech PO/ Talich: <u>Wood Dove</u>; <u>Golden Spinning Wheel</u>

Panton 01 0241. Czech PO/ Talich: <u>Midday Witch</u> (+ Smetana; Wagner)

Panton 010 239. Czech PO/ Talich: <u>Water Goblin</u>; <u>Wood Dove</u>

Artia ALP-178. Czech PO/ Talich: <u>Midday Witch</u>; <u>Golden Spinning Wheel</u> (+ Waltzes l, 4)

Urania URLP 7073. Czech PO/ Talich: <u>Midday Witch</u>; <u>Golden Spinning Wheel</u> (+ Waltzes l, 4)

Supraphon 1 10 1459. Czech PO/ Neumann: <u>Wood Dove</u> (+ Rhapsodies Nos. l-3)

Telefunken 6.35075. Czech PO/ Neumann: <u>Wood Dove</u> (+ <u>Czech Suite</u> etc) in "Tschechische Philharmonie" (three LP)

London CS 6979. Los Angeles PO/ Mehta: <u>Wood Dove</u> (+ Symphony No. 8)

Urania 7082. Berlin Radio SO/ Wissenhutter: <u>Water Goblin</u> (+ Kabalevsky; Prokofiev)

Supraphon 1 10 1889. Ostrava Janáček PO/ Trhlík: <u>Golden Spinning Wheel</u> (+ Janacek)

    Supraphon/ Gemini 1 SUPD 004 (+ Symphony No. 9; Janáček)

Urania 7010. SO of Radio Berlin/ Lehmann: <u>Wood Dove</u> (+ <u>Legends</u> Nos. 1-4, 7, 8)

Melodya D2255/56. Leningrad PO/ Rabinovich: <u>Wood Dove</u> (+ ?)

Legend LGDD 101. Czech PO/ Ančerl; Chalabala; Neumann; <u>Water Goblin</u>; <u>Midday Witch</u>; <u>Golden Spinning Wheel</u>; <u>Wood Dove</u> (+ <u>Heroic Song</u>) in "Orchestral Music of Dvorak, Vol I"

<u>Note</u>: Full texts to the four Erben tone poems (in Czech) accompany a Supraphon "Gramofonovy Klub" issue of 1963 accompanied by extensive analytical notes by Antonín Sychra. The tone poems are conducted by Zdeněk Chalabala with the Czech Philharmonic. Catalogue numbers: DV 5857, 5908, 6863 (three LP). This set is rounded off with five concert overtures conducted by Karel Ančerl.

HEROIC SONG (PISEN BOHATYRSKA), op.111 (B.199) (1899)

* Chandos CHAN 8597. Scottish National Orchestra conducted by Neeme Järvi (+ Symphony No. 1)

    Chandos ABRD 1291

* Supraphon CO-2196/97. Czech Philharmonic Orchestra conducted by Bohumil Gregor (+ Erben tone poems) (two CD)

    Supraphon 11-0201-1 033 (+ Erben tone poems; overtures "Nature, Love, Life")

* Opus 9150 1966/67. Slovak Philharmonic Orchestra conducted by Zdeněk Košler (+ Erben tone poems) (two CD)

    Opus 9110 1431/34 (+ Erben tone poems; <u>Symphonic Variations</u>) (four LP)

    MHS 830711

Dvořák's last piece for orchestra lies outside the Erben tone poem cycle, and stands apart as an enigma. Who is the hero? (Richard Strauss' <u>Ein Heldenleben</u> was completed two years later so does not serve as Dvorak's model.) Did specific personal or literary associations lie in the composer's mind?

Apparently Dvořák was probing new directions. Melodic ideas in <u>Heroic Song</u> come as terse phrases; moods shift rapidly with cyclic motives holding all together. Despite a most promising world premiere -- the Vienna Philharmonic led by Gustav Mahler -- Dvořák's farewell to the symphony orchestra still holds a Cinderella position on his works list.

Supplementary Recording:

> Legend LGDD 101. Prague Radio SO/ Klima (+ Erben tone poems; overtures "Nature, Love, Life," My Home; Symphonic Variations) (four LP)

Serenades, Dances and Suites:

SERENADE FOR STRINGS IN E MAJOR, op.22 (B.52) (1875)

SERENADE FOR WIND INSTRUMENTS, op.44 (B.77) (1878)

* LONDON 417 452-2. London Philharmonic Orchestra conducted by Christopher Hogwood

* Chandos CHAN 8459. Philharmonia Orchestra conducted by Christopher Warren-Green

    Chandos ABRD 1172

* Philips 400020-2. Academy of St.-Martin-in-the-Fields conducted by Neville Marriner

    Philips 6514145

* Academy Sound and Vision COE 801. Chamber Orchestra of Europe conducted by Alexander Schneider. Rec 1984

    * Musicmasters MMD 60095L

    Academy Sound and Vision COE 803

    MHS 7171 L

   The String Serenade ranks among Dvořák's most choice compositions, a work with melodic lines lovingly and poetically shaped. The five movements rest in perfect balance to offer sustained enchantment. The bracing Wind Serenade further exemplifies smooth adaptation of selected instrumental sonority, a work tracing ancestry back to the "harmony music" so prevalent in 18th-century Central Europe. Dvořák salts his rustic humor with touches of Czech folk dance, but his sophisticated technique elevates the Serenade high above mere diverting entertainment or pastiche.

Supplementary Recordings -- both Serenades:

* DGG 415364-2. Orpheus ChO/ Rec 1985

    DGG 415364

* Academy Sound and Vision ASV CD AS 6002. Northern Sinfonia of England/ Chung

    * Quicksilver CS AS 6002

    Angel AE-34448. English ChO; English Wind Ens/ Mackerras, Rec 1983

    EMI/Eminence EMX 2013

    Decca/Jubilee JB 87. London SO/ Kertész

    Supraphon SUA 10326. Prague Soloists O/ Talich; Professorium Conservatorii Pragensis Societas Cameralis

    Supraphon 50760. Czech ChO/ Vlach; Prague Ch Harmony/ Turnovsky Crossroads 22 16 1070

    Heliodor H3 25066. Hamburg Radio SO/ Schmidt-Isserstedt

Serenade for Strings, op.22:

* Supraphon CO-1788. Suk ChO/Suk (+ Suk)

* Supraphon/ Crystal Collection 11 0649-2. Prague ChO (+ Czech Suite)

    ProArte PAL 1033

    Hungaroton 12357. Liszt ChO/ Rolla (+ Tchaikovsky)

    London CS 6032. Israel PO/ Kubelik

    London/STS 15037

* DGG 400038-2. Berlin PO/ Karajan (+ Tchaikovsky)

    DGG 2532012

* Delos DCD 3011. Los Angeles ChO/ Gerard Schwarz (+ Silent Woods; Notturno)

   Delos DMS 3011

* Supraphon 11 0290 001. Orchestra of Prague Soloists/ Talich (+ Symphony No. 9)

* Rodolphe Productions RPC 2340. Musica da Praga/ Sagrestino (+ Waltzes, Nos. 1, 2; Notturno)

* Opus 9150 1501. Slovak ChO/ Warchal (+ Suk)

   Opus 9110 1501

* Novalis 150011-2. Camerata Bern (+ Sextet)

* Nimbus NI-5016. English String O/ Boughton (+ Tchaikovsky)

* ProArte DD 44. Utah SO/ Silverstein (+ Tchaikovsky)

   DGG 139 443. English ChO/ Kubelik (+ Kubelik)

* Erato ECD 55050. ChO of Lausanne/ Jordan (+ Czech Suite; Smetana)

   Erato NUM 75124

* Forlane UCD 16575. Ensemble Instrumentale de Grenoble/ Tardue (+ Tchaikovsky)

* Philips 422 031-2. Bavarian Radio SO/ C. Davis (+ Tchaikovsky)

   Philips 9500 105. English ChO; Leppard (+ Tchaikovsky)

   Philips 839 706. London SO/ C. Davis (+ Symphonic Variations)

   Supraphon 1 10 1653. Czech ChO/ Vlach (+ Suk)

   Erato STU 70792. Paillard ChO/ Paillard (+ Tchaikovsky)

   * The Compact Selection TQ 112

      MHS 3507

   Desmar DSM 1011. Royal PO/ Stokowski (+ Vaughan-Williams; Purcell)

   Turnabout 34532. Southwest German ChO/ Angerer (+ Janáček)

* MCA Classics MCAD 25889. Scottish ChO/ Laredo (+ Romance; Wagner)

* BIS CD 243 New Stockholm ChO/ Berglund (+ Tchaikovsky)

  Vanguard VSQ 30011. English ChO/ Somary (+ Tchaikovsky)

  Calliope 1618. Prague ChO/ Stejskal (+ Bagatelles)

  Classics for Pleasure CFP 40345. London PO/ Macal (+ Symphonic Variations)

  Angel S-37045. English ChO/ Barenboim (+ Tchaikovsky)

    Angel/Red Line RL-32084

* Laserlight 15 605. Berlin ChO/ Wohlert (+ Slavonic Dances, op.72)

Serenade for Winds, op.44:

* Orfeo C 051 831. Munich Wind Academy/ Brezina (+ Gounod) Rec 1981

* CRD 3410-2. Nash Ens (+ Krommer)

* Supraphon/Denon CO-2254. Prague Collegium Musicum; (+ Terzetto)

* MCA/Westminster MCA 1400. Musica Aeterna O/ Waldman (+ Czech Suite)

    Decca (USA) 71037

  Philips 6500 163. Netherlands Wind Ens/ De Waart (+ Gounod)

    Philips/Festivo 657025

  London CS 6594. Members of London SO/ Kertesz (+ Brahms)

    Decca/Jubilee JB 87

  Mercury MG 50041. Wind Section of Halle O/ Barbirolli (+ Haydn)

    Pye/Collector GSGC 2037

* Musicmasters MMD 60180H. Orchester der Beethovenhalle Bonn conducted by Dennis Russell Davis (– Bagatelles)

SLAVONIC DANCES, Series I, op.46 (B.83) (1878)

SLAVONIC DANCES, Series II, op.72 (B.137) (1887)

Op.46, No.1: furiant

2: dance variant of dumka

3: polka

4: sousedská (Czech waltz)

5: skočná (leap dance)

6: sousedská

7: skočná

8: furiant

Op.72, No.1: odzemek (Slovak variant of dumka)

2: mazurka with elements of dumka

3: skočná

4: Ukranian dumka

5: špacírka (Czech circle dance)

6: polonaise

7: kolo (Serbian round dance)

8: sousedská

* DGG/Galleria 419 056-2. Bavarian Radio Symphony Orchestra conducted by Raphael Kubelik

DGG 2530 466 (op.46) (+ Scherzo capriccioso)

DGG 2530 593 (op.72) (+ My Home)

* Supraphon/Treasury DC 8046. Czech Philharmonic Orchestra conducted by Karel Šejna

    Supraphon 50105/06 (two LP)

    Artia ALP 186/87 (two LP) (+ Smetana)

    * Supraphonet 11 1101-2011

* Enigma/Naxos 7 74670-2. Slovak Philharmonic Orchestra conducted by Zdeněk Košler

* Supraphon C37-7491. Czech Philharmonic Orchestra conducted by Václav Neumann

    Supraphon 1110 4711/12 (two LP)

* Chandos CHAN 8406. Scottish National Orchestra conducted by Neeme Järvi

    Chandos ABRD 1143

* London/Jubilee 417 749-2. Royal Philharmonic Orchestra conducted by Antal Dorati

    * London 411 735-2 (+ American Suite) (two CD)

    London 411 735-1 (+ American Suite) (two LP)

Dvořák composed the initial set of Slavonic Dances for piano four-hands, then almost immediately recast these eight gems into orchestral form. Phenomenal success put pressure on the composer for a second set; he delivered the sequel nine years later as op.72, also in piano and orchestral versions.

The first cluster (op.46) took cues from the Brahms Hungarian Dances, but probes deeper to assert the Bohemian-Moravian folk spirit. These infectious dance-derived fantasies are not arrangements; everything in them, tunes and all, comes entirely from Dvořák's boundless imagination. Backed by the Moravian Duets, these dances catapulted him to world fame.

The eight dances of the op.72 series are more complex emotionally and musically; wider reaches of the Slavic world are explored. Few composers have been able to match Dvořák at such a high level of folkish sophistication.

Supplementary Recordings:

* * Capriccio 10 229. Hungarian State O/ Fischer

* * Angel CDC 7 49547-2. Berlin PO/ Maazel

* * Philips 416623-2. Leipzig Gewandhaus O/ Masur

* * Supraphon/ Crystal Collection 11 0647-2 001. Czech PO/ Talich. Rec 1950

    Supraphon DV 5201/11 (two LP)

    Parliament PPL-221-2 (two LP)

    Urania 604 (two LP)

  Mercury OL-2-107. Minneapolis SO/ Dorati (two LP)

    Mercury MG 50335

    Wing SRW 18082

  Turnabout 34672. Bamberg SO/ Dorati

  Vanguard SRV 121 SD (VRS 495). Vienna State Opera O/ Rossi

    Vox SVUX 52001. Bamberg SO/ Perlea (two LP)

* * BIS 425. Rheinland-Pfalz PO/ Segerstam

  Supraphon 1110 2981/82. Czech PO/ Košler (two LP)

    ProArte 2020 (two LP)

    (Video Disc: Laser Disc MCO37U)

  Columbia MS 7208. Cleveland O/ Szell

    Odyssey Y2-33524 (two LP)

    Columbia M21-3226 (+ Carnival) (two LP)

    CBS 61089

  Epic SC-6015. Cleveland O/ Szell (+ Smetana arr Szell) (two LP)

* * BBC CD 731. Czech PO/ Talich. Rec in London 1936

Westminster XWN 18108/09. Philharmonic SO of London/Rodzinski (two LP). Note: The labeled orchestra is generally known as the Royal Philharmonic.

London LL-1283/84. Vienna PO/ Kubelik (+ Tchaikovsky) (two LP)

Telefunken 6.35075. Czech PO/ Neumann (+ _Czech_ _Suite;_ _Wood_ _Dove;_ _Rhapsodies_) (three LP)

Supplementary Recordings -- op.46:

* Teldec 8.44072. Czech PO/ Neumann (+ _Rhapsodies_ 2, 3)

* ProArte CDD 345. Houston SO/ Comissiona (+ _Carnival_)

* Marco Polo 8.223129. Slovak PO/ Košler (+ _Rhapsodies_ 1, 3)

  Fontana 698 024 CL. Vienna SO/ Ančerl (+ Brahms)

  RCA LM-2419. London SO/ Martinon (+ _Slavonic_ _Dances_ 72/7)

    RCA/Victrola 1054

  RCA LM-2096. Philharmonia O/ Malko (+ _Slavonic_ _Dances_ 72/1, 2)

  Everest 6104. Austrian SO/ Hagen (+ Smetana)

* LaserLite 15 635. Hungarian State O/ Fischer (+ Weber; Glinka)

* Philips 422 477-2. Concertegebouw O/ Haitink (+ Brahms)

Supplementary Recordings -- op.72:

* Teldec 842203. Czech PO/ Neumann (+ _Rhapsody_ No. 1)

* Marco Polo 8.223131. Slovak PO/ Košler (+ _Rhapsody_ _No._ _2;_ _Scherzo_ _capriccioso_)

  RCA/ Camden 284. Carlyle SO/ no conductor named. Note: This is possible LP repressing of Victor M-310 and M-345 with Czech PO under Václav Talich.

  Urania 7079. Czech PO/ Talich

* LaserLite 15 605. Berlin ChO/ Wohlert (+ Serenade, op.22)

Supplementary Recordings -- op.46 and 72, selections of two or more:

* Naxos/ Enigma Classics 7 74600-2. Czechoslovak Radio SO Bratislava/ Lenárd (+ Symphony No. 9)

* Naxos/ Enigma Classics D21E-74604. Slovak PO/ Wordsworth (+ Smetana)

* DGG 423206. Berlin PO/ Karajan (+ Symphony No. 9)

* London/Weekend Classics 417 696-2. Vienna PO/ Reiner (+ Brahms)

    London/STS 15009 (+ Brahms)

    London CM 9267/ CS 6198

    DGG 13080. Berlin PO/ Karajan (+ Brahms)

    DGG/Signature 2543509. Berlin PO/ Karajan (+ Smetana)

    London/STS 15409. Israel PO/ Kertesz (+ Smetana)

        London CM 9330/ CS 6330 (+ Smetana)

    London LL-779. Hamburg Radio SO/ Schmidt-Isserstedt (+ Brahms)

        Richmond B-19038

        London LD 9063 (ten-inch LP)

    Columbia ML 4785. Cleveland O/ Szell (+ Smetana). Arranged by George Szell

        Columbia ML 2023 (ten-inch LP)

    Richmond B-19030. London SO/ Kraus (+ Brahms)

    Telefunken 6.41964. London SO/ Boskovsky (+ Brahms)

    Classica CALS 112. Rome SO/ Scotti

    Telefunken/ Musik fur Alle NT 527. Bamberg SO/ Keilberth (+ Violin Concerto)

* Angel CDC 47618. Cleveland O/ Szell (+ Symphony No. 8)

        Angel S-36043

MHS 7189W. Leipzig Gewandhaus O/ Neumann (+ Brahms)

* DGG/Musikfest 413 251-2. Bavarian Radio SO/ Kubelik (+ Smetana) in "The Moldau." Op. 46/1-7; op.72/9-10.

Audio Spectrum ASC 846. Hamburg Philharmonic State O/ Muller-Lempertz (+ Liszt; Brahms)

LEGENDS, op.59 (B.122) (1881)

* BIS CD 436. Bamberg Symphony Orchestra conducted by Neeme Jarvi (+ Janáček)

* Nonesuch 79066-2 Rochester Philharmonic Orchestra conducted by David Zinman

   Nonesuch 79066-1

   Supraphon 1 10 1393 (10 1393-1 011). Brno State Philharmonic Orchestra conducted by Jiří Pinkas

Like the Slavonic Dances, the ten Legends began life in four-hand piano setting; orchestration came later. The set carries dedication to Vienna's fearsome critic Eduard Hanslick; both he and Brahms praised the piece for its profusion of charming ideas. Exactly what motivated Dvořák to compose these brief mood pictures spontaneously remains unclear. Where his Slavonic Dances vividly profile ethnic zest, Legends present the fires of folkish celebration glowing in the manner of banked coals. If concrete tales lie behind these delectable miniatures, the composer lets the riddle unwind entirely in the music.

Supplementary Recordings:

   Columbia ML 4920. Little O Society/ Scherman

   Supraphon DV 5274 (LPV 311). Czech PO/ Šejna

   DGG 2530 786. English CLO/ Kubelik

   Philips 6500188. London PO/ Leppard

   Urania 7010. Berlin Radio SO/ Lehmann (+ Wood Dove). Nos. 1, 2, 3, 4, 7, 8 only

   Pye Collector GGCD-304. Hallé O/ Barbirolli (+ Symphonies 7, 8, 9; Scherzo capriccioso) (two LP). Nos. 4, 6, 7 only

Concert Hall SMS 2322. Vienna Opera O/ Swarowsky (+ Cello Concerto). Nos. 4, 7 only

* CBC Enterprises SMCD-5039. Winnipeg SO/ Koizumi (+ Kodály; Morawetz; Tchaikovsky). No. 4 only

CZECH SUITE, op. 39 (B.93) (1879)

* Supraphon CO-73188. Prague Chamber Orchestra conducted by Oldřich Vlček (+ Janáček)

* Erato ECD 55050. Lausanne Chamber Orchestra conducted by Armin Jordan (+ Serenade, op.22; Smetana)

   Erato NUM 75124

* London 414 370-2. Detroit Symphony Orchestra conducted by Antal Dorati (+ Prague Waltzes; Notturno; Polka; Polonaise)

   London LDR 71024

* Nonesuch 79044-2. Los Angeles Chamber Orchestra conducted by Gerard Schwarz (+ Serenade, op.22)

   Nonesuch 79044-1

Three out of the five movements in the Czech Suite build upon folk dance material (polka, sousedska, furiant) which brings the piece close in style and idea to more Slavonic Dances. But overall design, conceived for small orchestra, leans more in the direction of a third serenade which actually seems to have crossed the composer's mind at the time. While not one of Dvořák's strongest scores, this neatly-proportioned, tuneful message wears well.

Supplementary Recordings:

Philips/Sequenza 6527129. English ChO/ Mackerras (+ Voříšek)

   Philips 6500 203

Westminster MCA-1400. Musica Aeterna O/ Waldman (+ Serenade, op.44)

   Decca (USA) 710137

* Koss Classics KC 1002. Milwaukee SO/ Macal (+ Symphony No. 8)

SUITE IN A MAJOR, "AMERICAN," op.98b (B.190) (1885)

* Virgin Classics VC 7 90723-2. Royal Liverpool Philharmonic Orchestra conducted by Libor Pešek (+ Symphony No. 9)

* London 411735-2. Royal Philharmonic Orchestra conducted by Antal Dorati (+ Slavonic Dances) (two CD)

Dvořák completed this suite while still a resident in New York, first for solo piano followed a year later by the orchestral version. This is attractive music, long on color and rhythm supplied by judicious dabs from the composer's Indian-Negro paintbox. The resultant Americana sounds uncontrived and convincing, sometimes taking on a languid quality reminiscent of the Florida impressions set to music about a decade before by Delius.

Supplementary Recordings:

* Nonesuch 79078-2. Rochester PO/ Zinman (+ Janáček)

    Nonesuch 79078-1

    Columbia ML-34513. Berlin Radio SO/ Thomas (+ American Flag)

PRAGUE WALTZES (PRAZKE VALCIKY) (B.99) (1879)

* Supraphon C-37-7922.   Prague Symphony Orchestra conducted by Jiří Bělohlávek in "Dvořák's Festival"

* London 414 370-2. Detroit Symphony Orchestra conducted by Antal Dorati (+ Polonaise; Czech Suite, etc)

    London LDA 71024

The chain of five Prague Waltzes derive from a ballroom need. They pose no threat to Johann Strauss.

POLKA IN B-FLAT MAJOR 'FOR PRAGUE STUDENTS,' op.53/A/1 (B.114) (1880)

* Supraphon C-37-7922.   Prague Symphony Orchestra conducted by Jiří Bělohlávek in "Dvořák's Festival"

* London 414-370-2. Detroit Symphony Orchestra conducted by Antal Dorati (+ Polonaise; Czech Suite etc)

POLONAISE IN E-FLAT MAJOR (B.100) (1879)

* Supraphon C-37-7922. Prague Symphony Orchestra conducted by Jiří Bělohlávek in "Dvořák's Festival"

* Opus/Allegro 9150 1189. Radio Bratislava Symphony Orchestra conducted by Ondrej Lenárd (+ Rusalka Polonaise; Tchaikovsky et al) in "Famous Orchestral Polonaises"

* London 414 370-2. Detroit Symphony Orchestra conducted by Antal Dorati (+ Czech Suite etc)

Supplementary Recording:

Oryx EXP 34. Prague SO/ Smetáček (+ Scherzo capriccioso; Smetana)

FESTIVAL MARCH (SLAVONSTI POCHOD), op.54 (B.88) (1879)

* Supraphon C37-7922. Prague Symphony Orchestra conducted by Jiří Bělohlávek in "Dvořák's Festival"

Panton 11 0361. Musici di Praga conducted by Václav Smetáček (+ Smetana et al) in "Festive Symphonic Marches"

Panton 8110 0069. Ministry of the Interior Band conducted by Vlastimil Kempe (+ Beethoven et al) in "Classic Marches"

Dvořák's Festival March, scored for full orchestra, pays an exuberant tribute in C Major to Emperor Franz Josef and his ill-fated Elizabeth on the occasion of their silver wedding celebrations. Unlike compatriots Julius Fučík and Karel Komzak, two of Austria-Hungary's most illustrious composers of military marches, Dvořák seemed to steer clear of the army and its musical needs. Yet there is a Franz Josef Marsch, possibly from the 1850's, among his dubious compositions (B.801).

Waltzes, op.54: see keyboard music and arrangements.

Miscellaneous Works for Orchestra:

SYMPHONIC VARIATIONS, op.78 (B.70) (1877)

* Supraphon/Gems 2SUP-0003. Czech Philharmonic Orchestra conducted by Václav Neumann (+ Symphony No. 9). Rec 1969

    Supraphon 1 10 0616 (+ Scherzo capriccioso; Notturno)

    Nonesuch H-71271

* London 417598. London Symphony Orchestra conducted by István Kertesz (+ Symphony No. 6)

    London CS 6721 (+ Golden Spinning Wheel)

* Chandos CHAN 8575. Scottish National Orchestra conducted by Neeme Järvi (+ Symphony No. 3; Carnival)

    Chandos ABRD 1270

* Angel CDB-62006. London Philharmonic Orchestra conducted by Zdenek Macal (+ Symphony No. 9)

The original theme behind these variations comes from Dvořák's choral song "I am a fiddler" composed the same year. He stretches the idea well beyond mere fiddle music, wasting no time in giving a formidable demonstration of the art of symphonic variations in twenty-eight pithy, closely-connected lessons. Events smartly move through a kaleidoscope of fast-shifting moods and tempos with a jaunty polka flashing past just before the fugal finale. No pedantry intrudes. This relatively early, but masterful opus lies on a par with Elgar's "Enigma" and Brahms' "Haydn" variations.

Supplementary Recordings:

* Hunt Productions CD-34017. NBC SO/ Toscanini (+ Smphony No. 9). Rec 1953

* Music and Arts Programs of America CD-287. Israel Pro-Musica O/ Atlas (+ Suk). Rec 1984

    Jerusalem ATD 8502 (+ Vaughan Williams)

* Philips 420349-2. London SO/ Colin Davis (+Symphony No. 9)

    DGG 253071/72. Bavarian Radio SO/ Kubelik (+ Midday Witch; Water Goblin)

Opus 9110 1431/33. Slovak PO/ Košler (+ Symphonic Poems) (three LP)

   MHS 837011W

Seraphim S-6003. Royal PO/ Sargent (+ Smetana) (two LP)

Columbia ML 4974. Royal PO/ Beecham (+ Balakireff)

Dell'Arte DA 9008. NBC SO/ Toscanini (+ Vivaldi; Rossini). Rec 1951

Supraphon LPV 109. Czech PO/ Šejna (+ Theme & Variations)

   Supraphon DV 5088

Classics for Pleasure CFP 40 345. London PO/ Macal (+ Serenade, op.22)

Philips PHS 900-196. London SO/ Colin Davis (+ Serenade, op.22)

MHS 4135. Czechoslovak Radio SO, Bratislava/ Slovak (+ Tchaikovsky)

   Opus 9111 0641

SCHERZO CAPRICCIOSO, op.65 (B.131) (1883)

* Chandos CHAN 8453. Ulster Orchestra conducted by Vernon Handley
  (+ overtures "Nature, Life, Love")

   Chandos SBRD 1163

* London 414 222-2. Cleveland Orchestra conducted by Christoph von Dohnányi
  (+ Symphony No. 8)

   London 414-222-1

* Angel CDC 49114. Philadelphia Orchestra conducted by Wolfgang Sawallisch
  (+ Symphony No. 9)

   EMI 49114

* London/Jubilee 417 742-2. London Symphony Orchestra conducted by István
  Kertesz (+ Symphony No. 9; Carnival)

   London CM 9358 (CS 6358; STS 15526) (+ Symphony No. 8)

* EMI/Laser CDZ 7 62514-2. Phiharmonia Orchestra conducted by Carlo Maria
  Giulini (+ Symphony 9; Carnival)

Unlike a light-hearted, capricious romp as the title might suggest, Dvořák's opus 65 is an expansive symphonic movement set down in almost defiant reaction at a time of personal crisis. Two sharply contrasted themes fight it out along a course punctuated by sudden modulations and abrupt restatement. With its seamless, lucid orchestration, Scherzo capriccioso rarely fails to produce a bracing listening experience.

Supplementary Recordings:

RCA LSC-3085. Philadelphia O/Ormandy (+ Smetana; Liszt)

Arturo Toscanini Recordings Association ATRA-3005. NBC SO?/ Toscanini (+ Cello Concerto). Rec 1940

Note: Recording includes rehearsal of Scherzo capriccioso.

* Telarc CD 80206. Los Angeles PO/Previn (+ Symphony No. 8; Notturno)

Supraphon 10 0616-1 011 (1110 0616). Czech PO/Neumann (+ Symphonic Variations; Notturno)

Nonesuch H-71271

Supraphon 11 0378-1 032. Czech PO/Gregor (Slavonic Rhapsodies; Symphonic Variations; My Home)

Angel SZ 37718. London PO/Rostropovich (Symphony No. 8)

Angel S-3870. Philharmonia O/Sawallisch (+ Symphony No. 8)

Angel S-3870. Dresden State O/Berglund (+ Slavonic Rhapsody No. 3; Smetana) (two LP)

DGG 2530466. Bavarian Radio SO/Kubelik (+ Slavonic Dances)

DGG 2530244. Berlin PO/Karajan (+ Weber et al)

Seraphim S-60098. Royal PO/Kempe (+ Smetana; Weinberger)

Mercury MG 50162. Hallé O/Barbirolli (+ Symphony No. 8)

Vanguard S-133

* DGG 423 220-2. Berlin PO/ Karajan (+ Smetana; Liszt)

NOCTURNE (NOTTURNO; NOKTURNO) IN B MAJOR FOR STRINGS, op.40 (B.47) (1875)

* London 414 370-2. Detroit Symphony Orchestra conducted by Antal Dorati (+ Czech Suite; Prague Waltzes; Polka; Polonaise)

    London LDA 71024

* Chandos CHAN 8223. London Philharmonic Orchestra conducted by Vernon Handley (+ Symphony No. 8)

    Chandos ABRD 1105

Vagrant melody subject to variational repetition in this curiously restless work -- even to the point of recalling early Schoenberg -- seems related to the composer's own ambiguity about the final form. He fussed over at least five reworkings, from a movement in an early string quartet (B.19), to part of a string quintet (B.49), a duet for violin and piano and so on up to the usually recorded version for string orchestra published in 1883. What may lie behind this music remains as elusive as ever. With Dvořák the answer is not always the obvious.

Supplementary Recordings:

* Rodolphe Productions RPC 2340. Musica da Praga/ Sagrestino (+ Serenade, op.22; Waltzes)

    Supraphon 1 10 0616. Czech PO/ Neumann (+ Scherzo capriccioso; Symphonic Variations)

    Nonesuch H-71271

    Angel DS-37758. Academy of St.-Martin-in-the-Fields/ Marriner (+ Wagner et al)

    Epic LC 3350. Boyd Neel O/ Dumont (+ Elgar et al)

* Telarc CD 80206. Los Angeles PO/ Previn (+ Symphony No. 8; Scherzo capriccioso)

SEVEN INTERLUDES (MEZIAKTNI SKLADBY) (B.15)

THREE NOCTURES (B.31)

FANFARES FOR FOUR TRUMPETS AND TIMPANI (B.167)

No recordings available.

Concerted works for Solo Instrument and Orchestra

Integrated Sets:

> Vox SVBX 5135. Piano Concerto; Violin Concerto; Cello Concerto No. 2;
> Mazurek; Rondo; Silent Woods. Rudolf Firkusny (p); Ruggiero Ricci
> (v); Zara Nelsova (vc); St. Louis Symphony Orchestra conducted by
> Walter Susskind (three LP)

> Supraphon 1110 3671. Piano Concerto; Violin Concerto; Cello Concerto
> No. 2. Ivan Moravec (p); Josef Suk (v); Josef Chuchro (vc); Czech
> Philharmonic Orchestra conducted by Jiří Bělohlávek; Václav Neumann
> (three LP)

> Supraphon 1 10 2081/82. Cello Concerto No. 1; Cello Concerto No. 2; Rondo;
> Polonaise; Silent Woods. Miloš Sádlo (c); Alfred Holeček (p); Czech
> Philharmonic Orchestra conducted by Václav Neumann (two LP)

PIANO CONCERTO IN G MINOR, op. 33 (B.63) (1876)

* London 417 802-2. Andras Schiff (p); Vienna Philharmonic Orchestra
  conducted by Christoph von Dohnanyi (+ Schumann)

* EMI/Angel CDC 747 667-2. Sviatoslav Richter (p); Bavarian State Orchestra
  conducted by Carlos Kleiber (+ Schubert)

  Angel S-37329

* Vox Prima MWCD 7114. Rudolf Firkusny (p); Saint Louis Symphony
  Orchestra conducted by Walter Susskind (+ Humoresques)

  * Mobile Fidelity MFCD 814

  Turnabout QTV 34691

* Supraphon/Treasury 8069. Radoslav Kvapil (p); Brno State Philharmonic
  Orchestra conducted by František Jilek (+ Violin Concerto)

  Supraphon 1110 2373

  * Supraphonet 11 1113-2 (+ Humoresques)

Initial performances of the Piano Concerto went well in Prague and London, but
Dvořák soon realized that practical problems existed in the solo part. He intended
to rectify these, but the task fell to others, notably Professor Vilém Kurz of the
Prague Conservatory. The posthumous Kurz edition served to keep the reputedly
impossible concerto "for two right hands" at least on the fringes of the repertoire.

A few advocates, notably Rudolf Firkusny, fought loyally for the work using various versions. More recently virtuosi the caliber of Sviatoslav Richter have helped demonstrate that any difficulties with Dvořák's original solo part could be overcome. Most recording pianists today seem to agree, so it seems that Dvořák was not a keyboard bungler after all.

Supplementary Recordings:

* Peters International PG PCD 7352. Bruno Rigutto (p); Orchestre Philharmonique de Radio France/ Macal

   Peters International PLE-102

* Koch-Schwann 316 003F 1. Justus Frantz (p); Northwest German P/ Muller-Bruhl

   Schwann/Musica Mundi VMS 2037

   MHS 3025H

   * MHS CD 316 003F

   Columbia M-33899. Justus Frantz (p); New York PO/ Bernstein

* Hunt CD 559. Sviatoslav Richter (p); London SO/ Kondrashin. Rec 1961

   Fonit Cetra DOC-27 (+ Chopin; Liszt) (three LP)

   Supraphon 1110 3030. Ivan Moravec (p); Czech PO/ Bělohlávek. Kurz version

   ProArte PAD 148

   Supraphon DV 5054. František Maxian (p); Czech PO/ Talich. Kurz version.

   Supraphon LPV 70

   Artia ALP-179

   Westminster Gold 8165. Rudolf Firkusny (p); Vienna State Opera O/ Somogyi. Rec 1963. Kurz version

   Westminster XWN   19044

   Columbia ML-4967. Rudolf Firkusny (p); Cleveland O/ Szell. Kurz-Firkusny version

   Odyssey Y-35210 (+ Tchaikovsky)

Turnabout TV-S 34539. Michael Ponti (p); Prague SO/ Rohan

Euphoria E-2028. Gregor Popovich (p); Nuremberg PO/ Toulier

Vox PL-7630. Friedrich Wührer (p); Vienna SO/ Moralt

* Melodram MEL 18029. Sviatoslav Richter (p); Czech PO/Smetáček (+ Bach; Chopin). Rec live 1954

    Period Showcase SHO 341. Sviatoslav Richter (p); Moscow National SO/Gauk

* AS Disc AS 536. Rudolf Firkusny (p); Philharmonic O/ Cantelli (+ Dukas; Roussel). Rec 1955

VIOLIN CONCERTO IN A MINOR, op.53 (B.96 and 108) (1879; revised 1880 and 1882)

* Angel CDC 7 749858-2. Kyung-Wha Chung (v); Philadelphia Orchestra conducted by Riccardo Muti (+ Romance)

* Angel CDC 47421-2. Nathan Milstein (v); New Philharmonia Orchestra conducted by Rafael Fruhbeck de Burgos (+ Goldmark)

    Angel S-36011 (+ Glazounov)

* Nonesuch 79052-2. Sergiu Luca (v); Saint Louis Symphony Orchestra conducted by Leonard Slatkin (+ Romance; Mazurek)

    Nonesuch 79052

* CBS MK 42257. Isaac Stern (v); Philadelphia Orchestra conducted by Eugene Ormandy (+ Brahms). Rec 1965

    Columbia MS-6876 (+ Romance)

    CBS M2-42338 (+ Lalo; Saint-Saens; Sibelius) (two LP)

* EMI CDH 7 63822 2. Yehudi Menuhin (v); Orchestre de la Societe des Concerts du Conservatoire, conducted by Georges Enesco (+ Mendelssohn; Wieniawski). Rec 1936

* Supraphon/ Treasury Series 8069. Josef Suk (v); Czech Philharmonic Orchestra conducted by Václav Neumann (+ Piano Concerto). Also 11 0701-2 (+ Suk)

  Supraphon 1410 2423 (+ Romance)

  ProArte PAL-1002 (+ Romance)

The popularity of the Dvořák Violin Concerto is astonishing, at least on records. Few critics would rank the piece alongside the monuments by Beethoven, Brahms or even Tchaikovsky. But the work does demonstrate undeniably attractive attributes: conciseness, a challeging solo role (brought to a high degree of polish upon the advice of Joseph Joachim) and abundant Czech-inflected melody notably the furiant-inspired rondo finale which crowns the work. As romantic excursions for violin with orchestra go, the taut, colorful A Minor Concerto rests among the gems of the repertoire.

Supplementary Recordings:

* CBS MH 44923. Midori (v) New York PO/ Mehta (+ Romance; Carnival). Rec live 1989

* DGG 419 618-2. Shlomo Mintz (v); Berlin PO/ Levine (+ Sibelius)

  DGG 419 618-1

* Angel CDC-47168-2. Itzhak Perlman (v); London PO/ Barenboim (+ Romance)

  Angel S-37069

  * Angel CMS 7 69881-2 (+ Mendelssohn et al) (two CD)

* Music and arts Programs of America CD-291. Herman Krebbers (v); Concertgebouw O/ Szell (+ Mozart; Wagner; Schumann; Richard Strauss). In album "The Best of George Szell" (Live concerts from 1965-1966)

* Movimento Musica 011 006. Isaac Stern (v); New York PO/ Mitropoulos (+ Cello Concerto). Rec 1951

* Vox Prima MWCD 7132. Ruggiero Ricci (v); Saint Louis SO/ Susskind (+ Mazurek; Romance; Smetana)

  London CM-9284/ CS-6215. Ruggiero Ricci (v); London SO/ Sargent (+ Tchaikovsky)

  London STS 15544

* Philips 420 895. Salvatore Accardo (v); Concertgebouw O/ Colin Davis (+ Sibelius)

   Philips 9500 406 (+ Romance)

* Acolade CL 50002. Herman Krebbers (v); Amsterdam PO/ Kersjes (+ Tchaikovsky)

* Panton CD 81 0855-2011. Václav Hudeček (v); Czech PO/Bělohlávek (+ Romance; Mazurek)

   Panton 11 0347. Václav Hudeček (v); Musici de Praga/ Smetáček (+ Mazurek). Rec 1972

   Supraphon 50181. Josef Suk (v); Czech PO/ Ančerl (+ Romance)

      Artia ALP-193

      Quintessence 2 PMC-2711 (+ Cello Concerto; Romance; Carnival) (two LP)

   * Supraphon/Crystal 11 0601-2 011 (+ Suk)

   * Fidelio 1840 (+ Romance)

   DGG 2535 391. Edith Peinemann (v); Czech PO/ Maag (+ Ravel)

      Heliodor 2548 227

   Vanguard 6016. David Oistrakh (v); Moscow Radio SO/ Kondrashin (+ Romance; Gliere)

      Vanguard 6027

      Melodya D 03064/5

   Angel/Melodya SR-40185. Viktor Pikaizen (v); Moscow Radio O/ Davd Oistrakh (+ Wieniawski)

      Chant du Monde LDX 78441 (+ Ysaÿe)

      Melodya D 023101/2

   Telefunken TC 8046. Joan Field (v); Berlin SO/ Rother (+ Beethoven)

      Telefunken/ Musik für Alle NT 527 (+ Slavonic Dances)

RCA LSC-3014. Itzhak Perlman (v); Boston SO/ Leinsdorf (+ <u>Romance</u>)

RCA/Gold Seal AGL1-1266

Colosseum O 582. Christine Raphael (v); Nuremberg SO/ Albert (+ Raphael)

* ProArte CCD-389. Joseph Silverstein (v); Utah SO/ Wilkins (+ Serenade, op.22)

* EMI CD-CFP 4566. Tamkin Little (v); Royal Liverpool PO/ Handley (+ Bruch)

<u>Note</u>: Additional recordings of the Violin Concerto, mostly on vintage LP, may be traced to: Bronislaw Gimpel (Vox PL 10290); Carmenzita Lozada (Eurodisc 80180); Tomas Magyar (Epic LC 3173); Nathan Milstein (RCA LM 1147) with Dorati; Nathan Milstein (Capitol P-8382) with Steinberg; Herman Krebbers (HMV Concert Series SXLP 30170); David Oistrakh (Colosseum 137); Riccardo Odnoposoff (Musical Masterpiece Society MMS-21); Johanna Martzy (DGG LPM 18152; Decca USA 9858)

ROMANCE IN F MINOR VOR VIOLIN AND ORCHESTRA, op.11 (B.39) (1873)

* Philips 420 168-2. Pinchas Zukerman (v); Saint Paul Chamber Orchestra led by Pinchas Zukerman (+ Beethoven; Schubert)

* Angel CDC-47168. Itzhak Perlman (v); London Philharmonic Orchestra conducted by Daniel Barenboim (+ Violin Concerto)

* Fidelio CD-1840. Josef Suk (v); Czech Philharmonic Orchestra conducted by Karel Ančerl (+ Violin Concerto)

* CBS MK 44823. Midori (v); New York Philharmonic Orchestra conducted by Zubin Mehta (+ Violin Concerto)

A delicious dividend frequently appended to recordings of the Violin Concerto, <u>Romance</u> is the expanded slow movement of an early string quartet (B.37). The recasting sounds appropriately soulful and entirely natural, a langorous charmer from start to finish.

<u>Supplementary Recordings</u>:

* Angel CDC 7 749858-2. Kyung-Wha Chung (v); Philadelphia / Muti (+ Violin Concerto)

* Nonesuch 7905-2. Sergiu Luca (v); Saint Louis SO/L. Leonard Slatkin (+ Violin Concerto; <u>Mazurek</u>)

* Panton CD 81 0855-2011. Václav Hudeček (v). Czech PO/ Bělohlávek
  (+ Violin Concerto; Mazurek)

  Supraphon 1410 2423. Josef Suk (v); Czech PO/Neumann (+ Violin
  Concerto)

    ProArte PAL-1002

* MCA MCAD-25889. Jaime Laredo (v); Scottish ChO/Laredo (+ Serenade),
  op.22)

  Columbia MS-6876. Isaac Stern (v); Philadelphia O/Ormandy (+ Violin
  Concerto)

  RCA/Gold Seal AGL1-1266. Itzhak Perlman (v); Boston SO/Leinsdorf
  (+ Violin Concerto)

  Also see works for violin and piano.

CAPRICCIO: CONCERT RONDO FOR VIOLIN AND ORCHESTRA, op.24
(B.421) (1878 ?)

  No recordings available.

MAZUREK FOR VIOLIN AND ORCHESTRA, op.49 (B.90) (1879)

* Nonesuch 79052-2. Sergiu Luca; Saint Louis Symphony Orchestra conducted
  by Leonard Slatkin (+ Violin Concerto; Romance)

* Vox Prima MWCD-7132. Ruggiero Ricci (v); Saint Louis Symphony Orchestra
  conducted by Walter Susskind (+ Violin Concerto; Romance; Smetana)

A Mazurek is said to be a Silesian variant of the Mazurka. The crisp, swirling
dance tune selected also brings out the sentimental side of Dvořák as he elegantly
develops it. Dedication reads to the famed Pablo Sarasate, also an expert in
transcribing exotic ethnic airs.

Supplementary Recordings:

  Panton 11 0347. Václav Hudeček (v); Musici de Praga/ Smetáček (+ Violin
  Concerto)

  Also see works for violin and piano.

CELLO CONCERTO NO. 1 IN A MAJOR (B.10) (1865)

* Supraphon/Treasury DC-8032. Miloš Sádlo (vc); Czech Philharmonic Orchestra conducted by Václav Neumann (+ Cello Concerto No. 2)

  * Supraphon/Gems 2SUP-0009 (+ Golden Spinning Wheel; Polonaise)

  Supraphon 1110 1718 (+ Polonaise)

  Supraphon 1 10 2081/82 (+ Cello Concerto No. 2; Polonaise); Silent Woods; Rondo in G Minor)

Like much of Dvořák's youthful production, his bold stab at a Cello Concerto might have ended up in the trash. He set down the solo instrument's part in full, but neglected to flesh out the orchestration. In 1925 a surviving piano score came to light, and Gunter Raphael reconstructed a performing version. For the first recording of this Dvořák rarity, however, Supraphon turned to an edition prepared by Miloš Sádlo with fresh, more idiomatic orchestration supplied by Jarmil Burghauser. Despite imbalances, thematic congestion and prolix solo writing, this hefty concerto shows a fertile musical mind at work. The determined honesty of this warmly romantic music (composed the same year as the First Symphony) commands admiration.

CELLO CONCERTO NO. 2 IN B MINOR, op. 104 (B.191) (1895)

* RCA/ Papillon Collection 6531-2-RG. Lynn Harrell (vc); London Symphony Orchestra conducted by James Levine (+ Schubert)

  RCA ARL1-1155

* Chandos CHAN 8662. Raphael Wallfisch (vc); London Symphony Orchestra conducted by Charles Mackerras (+ Dohnanyi)

  Chandos ABRD 1348

* DGG 413819-2. Mstislav Rostropovich (vc); Berlin Philharmonic Orchestra conducted by Herbert von Karajan (+ Tchaikovsky)

  DGG 139044

  DGG/Galleria 2543 054

* Supraphon CO-1152. Angelica May (vc); Czech Philharmonic Orchestra conducted by Václav Neumann (+ Martinu)

  Supraphon 1110 3623

* Angel CDC 47614. Jacqueline Du Pré (vc); Chicago Symphony Orchestra conducted by Daniel Barenboim (+ Haydn)

    Angel S-36046 (+ Silent Woods). Rec 1971

* DGG/ Galleria 423 881-2. Pierre Fournier (vc); Berlin Philharmonic Orchestra conducted by George Szell (+ Elgar)

    DGG 138755 (+ Bruch)

This king of all cello concertos derived from Dvořák's American sojourn, yet differs from companion pieces like the "New World" Symphony in being relatively oblivious to locale. He completed the concerto upon return to Bohemia, where deeply saddened by the death of his beloved sister-in-law Josefina Kaunitzová, he made significant changes in the score as a tribute to her memory. The idea to compose a cello concerto in the first place, however, goes back to requests from Dvořák's cellist friend Hanuš Wihan, with strong reinforcement from hearing Victor Herbert's noteworthy contribution to the repertoire in his Cello Concerto No. 2 (Angel CDC 7 47622-2). Soloists quickly took up Dvořák's concerto and since have kept it in forefront position. Nearly all the great names in the cellists' community have gradually added their performances to records, so the pre-LP trickle has since become a flood.

Supplementary Recordings:

* Philips 422 387-2. Julian Lloyd Webber (vc); Czech PO/ Neumann (+ Rusalka Polonaise; Carnival). Rec 1988

* BIS CD-245. Frans Helmerson (vc); Gothenberg SO/ Järvi (+ Rondo; Silent Woods).

* CBS IM-42206. Yo-Yo Ma (vc); Berlin PO/ Maazel (+ Rondo; Silent Woods). Also M2K 44562 in "Great Cello Concertos" (two CD)

    CBS IM-42206

* Philips 412880-2. Heinrich Schiff (vc); Concertgebouw O/ Colin Davis (+ Elgar). Rec 1980

    Philips 6514071 (+ Silent Woods)

* Philips/ Concert Classics 422 467-2. Maurice Gendron (vc); London PO/ Haitink (+ Rondo; Faure)

    Philips 802892 LY (+ Rondo; Silent Woods); Festivo 6570 112

* Philips/Legendary Classics 420 776-2. Emanuel Feuermann (vc); National Orchestral Association/Barzin (+ Silent Woods; Rondo; Bloch). Rec 1940

* Supraphon DC-8032. Josef Chuchro (vc); Czech PO/ Neumann (+ Cello Concerto No. 1)

* Vox Prima MWCD-7131. Zara Nelsova (vc); Saint Louis SO/ Susskind (+ Rondo; Silent Woods; Smetana)

* London 410144-2. Lynn Harrell (vc); Philharmonia O/ Ashkenazy (+ Bruch)

  London LDR-71108

* Nimbus 5127. Alexander Michejew (vc); London SO/ Boughton (+ Saint-Saens)

* Angel CDC 49306. Mstislav Rostropovich (vc); London PO/ Giulini (+ Saint-Saens)

    Angel S-37457

* Erato ECD 88224. Mstislav Rostropovich (vc); Boston SO/ Ozawa (+ Tchaikovsky)

    Erato NUM 75282

* Movimento Musica 011 006, Antonio Janigro (vc); Cologne Radio SO/ Erich Kleiber (+ Violin Concerto). Rec 1955

* Philips CD/MC 420 873-2. Janos Starker (vc); London SO/ Dorati (+ Schumann)

    Mercury 75045 (+ Bruch)

  Seraphim S-60136. Mstislav Rostropovich (vc); Royal PO/ Boult. Rec 1958

    HMV SXLP 30176

  RCA LSC-2490. Gregor Piatigorsky (vc); Boston SO/ Munch

    RCA AGL1-3878

    RCA AGL1-5265 (digital remastering)

  Columbia ML-4022. Gregor Piatigorsky (vc); Philadelphia O/ Ormandy

    Odyssey Y 34602

  Arturo Toscanini Recording Association ATRA-3005, Kurtz (vc); NBC SO(?)/Toscanini (+ Scherzo capriccioso). Rec 1945

Columbia MS-6714. Leonard Rose (vc); Philadelphia O/ Ormandy
(+ Tchaikovsky)

CBS 61036

* Hungaroton HCD 12868. Miklos Perényi (vc); Budapest Festival O/ Fischer
(+ Tchaikovsky)

Hungaroton SLPX 11866

Fidelio 3327

* DGG 427 347-2. Mischa Maisky (vc); Israel PO/ Bernstein (+ Bloch)

Supraphon SUA 10125. Mstislav Rostropovich (vc); Czech Philharmonic O/
Talich. Rec 1952

Quintessence PMC-7142 (+ Carnival)

Parliament PLP-139

Supraphon SUA 10404/05. Portion of live rehearsal, in "Václav Talich and
The Czech Philharmonic" (two LP)

Angel/ Eminence AE-34458. Paul Tortelier (vc); London SO/ Previn
(+ Tchaikovsky)

EMI/Angel ASD 3652 (+ Rondo)

Angel S-35417. Janos Starker (vc); Philharmonia O/ Susskind (+ Fauré)

Classics for Pleasure CFP 40361. Robert Cohen (vc); London PO/Macal

Philips 6500224. Christine Walevska (vc); London PO/ Gibson
(+ Tchaikovsky)

Philips/Sequenza 6527052

Music Minus One 353. Absent solo part; Stuttgart SO/ Kahn

King Records K33Y-239. Gary Karr (db); Osaka PO/ Asahina. Transcription
for double bass

* Panton CD 81 076 2031. Michaela Fukačová (vc); Prague SO/ Bělohlávek

* Balkaton 030026. Anatoli Krustev (vc); Plovdiv PO/Dimitrov (+ Haydn)

Additional Recordings by Cellist Mstislav Rostropovich (derived from Melodya original LP masters):

> MHS 7035; Monitor S-2090 (cond. Khaikin)
> Melodya D 0566/7; Hall of Fame HOFS-523 (cond. Rachlin)
> Sine Qua Non SQN 7754 (cond. Samosud)
> Westminster/ Gold WGM-8245 (cond. Khaikin)
> Period/ Showcase SHO ST 2334 (cond. Rachlin)

Additional Recordings by Other Cellists:

Antonio Janigro (Westminster XWN 18517); Antonio Menezes (Melodya 10 00015/6; Zara Nelsova (London LLP 537); Gaspar Cassado (Vox PL-9360); Tibor de Michula (Epic LC 3883); Pierre Fournier (London LL-1106); Enrico Mainardi (DGG 18 236/ Heliodor 478 442); Paul Tortelier (Musical Masterpiece Society MMS-2006); Paul Tortelier (HMV SXLP 30018); Ludwig Hoelscher (Telefunken TCS 18022); Walter Nothas (Camerata CMT-1005); Saša Vectomov (Supraphon 1 10 2084); Anatole Krustev (Balkanton 30026); Bernard Greenhouse (Concert Hall SMS 2322); André Navarra (Capitol P-8301); Georg Metzger (Saphir 25747-75B); ? Mann (Artisico YD 3010); M. Predelya (Melodya SM 03467/8); L. Parnas (Melodya DO 10589/90); Emanuel Feuermann (opal 809).

The Historic Recording from 1937 by Pablo Casals, With Czech Philharmonic Orchestra, conducted by George Szell:

> HMV Album 306 (Victor M-458) (78 rpm)
> Victor LCT-1026
> Angel COLH-30
> Seraphim 60240
> * Pearl GEMM CD 9349
> * EMI/Angel References CDH 7 63498-2
> Franklin Mint Recording Society 41/42 (+ Brahms et al) (two LP)

RONDO IN G MINOR FOR CELLO AND ORCHESTRA, op.94 (B.181) (1893)

* Academy Sound and Vision CDRPO 8012. Paul Tortelier (vc); Royal Philharmonic Orchestra conducted by Charles Groves (Elgar; Tchaikovsky)

    * MCA 6295-2

* BIS CD 245. Frans Helmerson (vc); Gothenburg Symphony Orchestra conducted by Neeme Järvi (+ Cello Concerto; Silent Woods)

* CBS IM-42206. Yo-Yo Ma (vc); Berlin Philharmonic Orchestra conducted by Lorin Maazel (+ Cello Concerto; Silent Woods)

* Vox Prima MWCD-7131. Zara Nelsova (vc); Saint Louis Symphony Orchestra conducted by Walter Susskind (+ Cello Concerto; Silent Woods; Smetana)

Intended as an encore vehicle for Hanuš Wihan, a close friend and the leading Czech cellist of Dvořák's time, Rondo crops up frequently to supplement the Cello Concerto on records. This perky piece takes immediate hold melodically, and the slight ideas are treated imaginatively.

Supplementary Recordings:

* EBS 6059. Julius Berger (vc); National Polish Radio SO/ Straszynski (+ Silent Woods; Elgar; R. Strauss)

* Danacord DACOCD 330. Niels Ullner (vc); Malmo SO/ Westerberg (+ Bruch et al) in album "Cello Favorites"

  Also see works for cello and piano.

SILENT WOODS (WALDESRUHE; KLID), op.68 No. 5 (B.182) (1893)

* CBS MK 42206. Yo-Yo Ma (vc); Berlin Philharmonic Orchestra conducted by Lorin Maazel (+ Cello Concerto; Rondo)

* Delos DCD-3011. Douglas Davis (vc); Los Angeles Chamber Orchestra conducted by Gerard Schwarz (+ Serenade, op.44)

* Vox Prima MWCD-7131. Zara Nelsova (vc); Saint Louis Symphony Orchestra conducted by Walter Susskind (+ Cello Concerto; Rondo Smetana)

* BIS CD 245. Frans Helmerson (vc); Gothenburg Symphony Orchestra conducted by Neeme Järvi (+ Cello Concerto; Rondo)

Relatively popular among Dvořák's lesser items, Silent Woods is the composer's arrangement for cello with orchestra/piano of the fifth movement from his duo piano cycle From the Bohemian Forest. The result is a routine romantic reverie but one well-suited for the cello's throaty timbre.

Supplementary Recordings:

* EBS 6059-2. Julius Berger (vc); Polish National Radio SO/ Straszynski (+ Rondo; Elgar; R. Strauss)

* Philips 420776-2. Emanuel Feuermann (vc); National Orchestra Association/ Barzin (+ Cello Concerto; Rondo; Bloch)

Angel S-36046. Jacqueline Du Pré (vc); Chicago SO/ Barenboim (+ Cello Concerto)

Philips/ Festivo 6570 112. Maurice Gendron (vc); London PO/ Haitink (+ Cello Concerto; Rondo)

Also see works for cello and piano.

IV

Chamber Music

<u>Integrated Sets</u>:

Vox SVBX 549. Five String Quartets: opp. 16, 34, 51, 61, 90/27. Kohon Quartet of New York University. In "Dvořák Chamber Music" Vol. I (three LP)

Vox SVBX 550. Four String Quartets: opp. 2, 96 ("American"),   105, 106. Kohon Quartet. Volume II (three LP)

Vox SVBX 551. Piano Quintet in A, op.81; <u>Twelve Cypresses</u>; String Quartet in B-flat, op.17; Double-Bass Quintet in G, op.77/18. The Berkshire Quartet with Gyorgy Sandor (p) and Murray Grodner (db). Volume III (three LP)

Vox SVBX 571. Piano Trios No. 1 in B-flat; No. 4 in E minor ("Dumky"); Piano Quartets No. 1 in D, op.23; No. 2 in B-flat, op.87; <u>Bagatelles</u>. The Dumka Trio with Walter Gerhart (va) and John Willison (v). Volume IV (three LP)

Vox SVBX 588. Two String Quintets, opp. 1 and 97; Two Piano Trios, opp.26 and 65; <u>Two Waltzes</u> (arr String Quartet), op.54; String Sextet, op.48. The Austrian String Quartet with Imgard Schuster (va) and Dankwart Gahl (vc). Volume V (three LP)

* DGG 429 193-2. Compositions for string quarter (complete). The String Quartets 1-14; <u>Twelve Cypresses</u>; Quartet Movement (c1873); <u>Quartet Fragment in F</u> (1881; B.120); <u>Two Waltzes</u>. Prague Quartet (nine CD)

   DGG 2740177 (twelve LP)

Quintets:

STRING QUINTET IN A MINOR, op.1 (B.7) (1861)

Philips SAL 3765 (839 754LY). Members of the Berlin Philharmonic Octet (+ Sextet)

Vox SVBX 588. Austrian String Quartet, with Imgard Schuster (2nd va) in "Dvorak Chamber Music" Vol V

Composed at age 19, Dvořák's official opus one did not see performance during his lifetime. The piece dispenses with the expected scherzo, but otherwise takes cue from the Vienna tradition. There is, however, unusual construction supporting this genial music which Dvořák handles with commendable assurance.

STRING QUINTET IN G MAJOR WITH DOUBLE BASS, op.77/18 (B.49) (1875)

* Arabesque Z-6558. Portland String Quartet with Gary Karr (db) (+ String Quartet No. 12)

* Dynamic CDS-45. Accardo (v); M. Batjer (v); T. Hoffman (va); P. Wiley (vc) with F. Petracchi (db) (+ Terzetto). Rec 1986

Thorofon/Cappella MTH 255. Frankfurt Philharmonic Ensemble

With the standard string quartet reinforced at the bottom by a double-bass (instrumentation not followed by many composers) the cello is released for more interesting duties along with enrichment of the usual string ensemble sound. This was one of the first works to establish the distinctive cut of Dvořák's musical personality, and the melodic flow of this warm composition throws off many passages born of ethnic feeling. The preferred opus number is 18, not 77 as originally published. An extra movement, subsequently discarded by the composer (published as a supplement in the Complete Edition) resurfaced as the Nocturne for Strings, op.40.

Supplementary Recordings:

Westminster XWN 18066. Vienna Konzerthaus Quintet (+ Sonata; Romantic Pieces)

Westminster WL 50-26 (Quintet only)

DGG 2350214. Boston Symphony Chamber Players, Original five-movement version

MHS 7462. Saint Lukes Chamber Ensemble (+ Doppler)

Supraphon 50186. Dvořák Qt with Pošta (db)

Repeat 250-3. Berry (v); Sosson (v); Kievmen (va); Rehrer (vc); Bundock (db)

Vox SVBX 551. Berkshire Qt with Grodner (db) in "Dvořák Chamber Music" Vol III

STRING QUINTET IN E-FLAT, op.97 (B.180) (1893)

* Denon CO-72507. Smetana Quartet with Josef Suk (va) (+ Quintet, op.5)

    Supraphon 1111 2179. Smetana Quartet with Josef Suk (va) (+ Silent Woods)

    MHS 4842

    ProArte PAL-1074

* Hyperion CDA 66308. Raphael Ensemble (+ Sextet)

Sketched and score completed at Spillville, Iowa, the E-flat String Quintet is one of the most American-sounding works from the composer's American period. Exuberance lies everywhere with vivid themes and animated rhythms possibly stylized by Dvořák's limited contact with groups of Indians and their music. The slow movement, a set of five variations on an idea apparently jotted down even before the journey to America, is superb. In any event, the old world and the new blend happily.

Supplementary Recordings:

Supraphon 50684. Dvořák Qt with Josef Kodousek (va) (+ Cypresses)

    Crossroads 22 16 0082

RCA ARL1-1791. Guarneri Qt with Walter Trampler (va) (+ String Quartet No. 12)

Columbia MS-6952. Budapest Stg Qt with Walter Trampler (va) (+ Beethoven)
    Columbia M 32792 (+ String Quartet no. 12)

Columbia ML-4799. Budapest Stg Qt with Milton Katims (va) (+ Brahms)

London/STS 15438. Vienna Philharmonia Quintet (+ Bagatelles)

London/STS 15242. Members of Vienna Octet (+ Sextet)

Vox SVBX 588. Austrian Stg Qt with Schuster (va). In "Dvořák Chamber Music" Vol V

Philips 6500363. Berlin Philharmonic Quintet (+ Piano Quintet)

Westminster 17099. European Qt with Strabl (va) (+ Sextet)

PIANO QUINTET IN A MAJOR, op.5 (B.28) (1872)

* Denon CO-72507. Smetana Quartet with Jan Panenka (p) (+ String Quintet, op.97)

    Supraphon 10 4115 (+ Piano Quintet, op.81)

* Philips 412429-2. Borodin Quartet with Sviatoslav Richter (p) (+ Piano Quintet, op.81). Rec live 1982

    Philips 412429-1 (two LP)

The earliest of Dvořák's two piano quintets came close to oblivion when the composer destroyed the autograph score sometime after the first performance in Prague. In 1887, however, Dvořák retrieved a friend's copy to make substantial cuts and other changes. While the newborn quintet does not measure up to major Dvořák, the piece sounds well in revision and was worth salvaging. Most of the rhythmic interest centers in the last of three movements.

PIANO QUINTET IN A MAJOR, op.81 (B.155) (1887)

* Philips 412419-2. Borodin Quartet with Sviatislav Richter (p) (+ Piano Quintet, op.5)

    Philips 412 429-1 (two LP)

* Denon C37-7338. Smetana Quartet with Josef Hála (p) (+ String Quartet No. 12)

* Denon CO-1329. Smetana Quartet with Jan Panenka (p) (+ Schumann)

* RCA/ Gold Seal 7965-2-RG. Jascha Heifetz (v); Israel Baker (v); Joseph de Pasquale (va); Gregor Piatigorsky (vc); Jacob Lateiner (p) (+ Brahms)

    RCA LSC-2985 (+ Francaix)

* Vanguard VCD 72028. Alexander Schneider (v); Felix Galimir (v); Michael Tree (va); David Soyer (vc); Peter Serkin (p) (+ Mozart)

* RCA/ Gold Seal 6263-2. Guarneri Quartet with Artur Rubinstein (p) (+ String Quartet No.12)

    RCA LSC-3252

* Ex Libris CD-6042. Zurich Chamber Players with Werner Bartschi (p) (+ Martinu)

* CBS/ Masterworks MK 44920. Tokyo String Quartet with Hiroko Nakamura (p) (+ String Quartet No. 12)

* Virgin Classics VC 7 90736-2. Nash Ensemble with Jan Brown (p) (+ Piano Trio, op.90)

* ProArte CDD 470. The Soloists of the Vienna Chamber Orchestra with Philippe Entremont (p) (+ Schubert)

* Dynamic CD 51. Salvatore Accardo(v) and Colleagues (+ Four Romantic Pieces)

Mercurial moods, melodic fertility, sure grasp of tectonics spiced by a touch of Slavic color -- all the attributes that make Dvořák sound like Dvořák -- concentrate in this meaty masterpiece. Opus 81 marks one of the supreme achievements in his art, a salient example of perfection in chamber music.

Supplementary Recordings:

* Arabesque 26613. ProArte Qt; Artur Schnabel (p) (+ Schumann). Rec 1934 (Victor album VM-219)

    Bruno Walter Society BWS-718

* IVC/ Melodya 1046. Borodin Qt; Richter (p). Rec live 1983

    Melodya 10 00067 001

    Le Chant du Monde LDX 78786 (+ Terzetto)

* London 421 153-2. Vienna Philharmonic Qt; Curzon (p) (+ Franck)

    London CS-6357

    Ace of Diamonds SDD 270 (+ Schubert)

    Vox SVBX 551. Berkshire Qt; Sándor (p) (three LP)

    Turnabout 34075-S (+ Trio, op.90)

Philips 6500 363. Members of Berlin Octet; Bishop (p) (+ String Quintet, op.97)

RCA ARL1-2240. Cleveland Qt; Ax (p)

CBS M-34515. Julliard Qt; Firkusny (p) (+ Bagatelles)

Columbia ML-4825. Budapest Qt; Curzon (p)

Westminster XWN-18519. Barylli Qt; Farnadi (p) (+ Quartet No. 14)

Westminster WL 5337

Mars 207803. Philharmonisches Kammerensemble Berlin; Cappone (p) (+ Arensky)

Muza SXL-0639. The Warsaw Quintet

Concert Disc CS-251. Fine Arts Qt with Glazer (p)

Supraphon LPV-114.   Smetana Qt with Panenka (p) (+ Humoresque; Mazurek)

Supraphon DV 5610

London LL 202. Chigi Quintet

Ace of Clubs 277

Mercury 10043. Ondríček Qt with Herman (p) (from Esta 78 rpm H-5027/30)

HMV ASD 2350. Smetana Qt with Štepán (p) (+ String Quartet No. 6)

Sextet:

STRING SEXTET IN A MAJOR, op.48 (B.80) (1878)

* Denon CO-72540. Smetana Quartet with Josef Suk (va) and Josef Chuchro (vc) (+ String Quartet No. 12)

* Chandos CHAN 8771.   Academy of St. Martin-in-the-Fields Chamber Ensemble (+ Martinu)

* Hyperion CDA 66308. Raphael Ensemble (+ String Quintet, op.97)

* Elektra/Nonesuch 9 79128-2. Boston Symphony Chamber Players (+ Smetana)

* Calliope CAL 7217. Talich Quartet with Jiří Najnar (va) and Václav Bernasek (vc) (+ Schoenberg)

* Campion Records RRCD 1301. Camerata Nova (+ Bagatelles)

* Novalis 150 011-2. Camerata Bern (+ Serenade, op.22)

A classic in the limited supply of extended works for six string players, Dvořák's sunny contribution indulges in folk dance inspiration to sustain a bucolic atmosphere. Composed soon after the Slavonic Dances, the ethnic zest continues down to passing quotation. This attractive work did much to help cement Dvořák's international reputation.

Supplementary Recordings:

Supraphon 50824. Dvořák Qt with members of Vlach Qt (+ Miniatures)

Philips SAL 3765 (839 754 LY). Members of Berlin Octet (+ Quintet, op.1)

London/STS 15242. Members of Vienna Octet (+ Quintet, op.97)

Remington 199-12. Jilka Sextet

Westminster 17099. European Qt with Strabl (v); Herzer (vc) (+ Quintet, op.97)

Vox SVBX-588. Austrian Stg Qt with Schuster (v); Gahl (vc) (three LP)

Quartets:

STRING QUARTET NO. 1 IN A MAJOR, op.2 (B.8) (1862); rev 1888)

Vox SVBX 550. Kohon Quartet. In "Dvořák Chamber Music" Vol. II

DGG 2740 117. Prague Quartet. In complete string quartets.

The situation surrounding the string quartets of Antonin Dvořák parallels what once prevailed with his symphonies: a general ignorance of material, mostly unpublished in the composer's lifetime, preceding what long had been established in the standard repertoire. Renumbering obviously became necessary, so as the symphonies now number nine, the quartets for strings come to a total of fourteen.

In the case of the A Major Quartet, op.2, Dvořák pruned a prolix indulgence from his twenty-first year just before a belated first performance in 1888. Approximately 100 bars came off both ends; both middle movements largely stayed intact. The slimmed-down result is appealing in its cheerfulness, and amounts to more than a mere historical curiosity. The notable scherzo evidently is the first of its kind from the composer's hand.

STRING QUARTET NO. 2 IN B-FLAT MAJOR B.17 (1870)

Vox SVBX 551. Berkshire Quartet. In "Dvořák Chamber Music" Vol. III

DGG 2740 117. Prague Quartet. In Dvořák String Quartets (complete)

In original form, what is now held to be Dvořák's Second String Quartet tended to long-windedness under a Wagnerian spell, and ran on rhapsodically for about 50 minutes. Dvořák never sought publication or revision; editorial deletion to create a reasonable performing version is the work of other hands. Dvořák evidently considered the quartet an experiment in fluid form and applied chromatic harmony as practiced in Beyreuth. Publication only came in 1962.

STRING QUARTET NO. 3 IN D MAJOR (B.18) (1870)

STRING QUARTET NO. 4 IN E MINOR (B.19) (1870)

STRING QUARTET NO. 5 IN F MINOR (B.37), op.9 (1873)

STRING QUARTET NO. 6 IN A MINOR (B.40), op.12 (1873)

DGG 2740 117. Prague Quartet. In complete string quartets.

* DGG 429 1932

The Third through Sixth String Quartets long lay in unpublished darkness. They document, with a profusion of ideas sometimes out of firm control, Dvořák's years of unrecognized artistic struggle and Wagnerian influence.

Quartet No. 3 plays longer than most of Bruckner's vast symphonies. Number 4 spins out a web of chromaticism in one continuous movement. Single-movement construction comes again in No. 6 (a revised version, left unfinished by the composer, settles for four movements). The manuscript for No. 5 has vanished and owes its shaky existence to a questionable revision by Günther Raphael.

Entry even to the fringes of the string quartet repertoire is unlikely for these rarities; all the more reason to hope for wider circulation in recorded form.

STRING QUARTET NO. 7 IN A MINOR, op.16 (B.45) (1874)

    ProArte PAD 132. Varsovia Quartet (+ Quartet No. 12)

    Vox STPL 516.360. Kohon Quartet (+ Quartet No. 12)

      Vox SVBX 549. "Dvořák Chamber Music" Vol. III

    DGG 2740 112. Prague Quartet (with complete quartets)

Dvořák's first example of chamber music to find publication sees him on firm ground with prolixity a thing of the past. All flows agreeably as he advances towards mastery of this difficult medium.

STRING QUARTET NO. 8 IN E MAJOR, op.80/27 (B.57) (1876)

    Supraphon 50528. Dvořák Quartet (+ <u>Waltzes</u>)

      Crossroads 22 16 0090

    Vox SVBX 549. Kohon Quartet, "Dvořák Chamber Music" Vol. I

    DGG 2530 719. Prague Quartet (+ Quartet No. 10)

      DGG 2740 112 (with complete quartets)

*   Chandos CHAN 8755. Chillingirian Quartet (+ Quartet No. 9)

Opus 27 (not op.80 as originally published) is neat, lucid and beautifully balanced. More than a hint of sadness comes from modulations into minor keys. As often occurs in Dvořák, the slow movement is wistfully distinctive.

STRING QUARTET NO. 9 IN D MINOR, op.34 (B.75) (1877)

*   Nonesuch 79126-2. American String Quartet (+ Quartet No. 10)

*   Chandos CHAN 8755. Chillingirian Quartet (+ Quartet No. 7)

About the time of composition, Dvořák's fortunes were on the rise, due in no small way, to the selfless support of Brahms. A grateful Dvořák dedicated this quartet to him. To this tribute is attached a splendid, lithe work which pays due respect to Vienesse ancestors. But the polka-touched Second Movement, like the vigorous finale, shows the stamp "Made in Bohemia."

Supplementary Recordings:

London CM 9394. Janáček Qt (+ Quartet No. 12)

London/STS 15207

Pierre Verany PV 83095/CA 682. Quatuor de Provence (+ Quartet No. 12)

Supraphon 50529. Smetana Qt (+ Martinů)

Artia ALPS 717

Vox SVBX 549. Kohon Qt in "Dvořák Chamber Music" Vol I

DGG 2740 112. Prague Qt (in complete quartets)

STRING QUARTET NO. 10 IN E-FLAT MAJOR, op.51 (B.92) (1879)

* Denon C37-7235. Kocian Quartet (+ Quartet No. 14)

* Supraphon C37-7910. Panocha Quartet (+ Quartet No. 13)

* Nonesuch 79126-2/ American String Quartet (+ Quartet No. 9)

    Nonesuch 79126-1

* Cadenza CAD 973-8. Stamitz Quartet (+ Quartet No. 14)

* Teldec 8.43105. Vermeer Quartet (+ Verdi)

    Teldec 43105

The truly distinguished line of Dvořák's string quartets begins with opus 51, and from here on never wavers. The E-flat Major Quartet is a singularly handsome offering brimming with vitality and Slavic color The gentle rocking figure at the opening brings one of his most inspired movements, while the second movement provides an excellent example of his way with the dumka with its characteristic clouds and sunshine contrasts. In the Finale come more specific Czech references to the sprightly folk dances -- the furiant and skočna.

Supplementary Recordings:

    Centaur 1008/9. New World Qt (+ Quartets Nos. 12 and 14) (two LP)

    DGG 2530 719. Prague Qt (+ Quartet No. 8)

      DGG 2740 117 (with complete string quartets)

    Supraphon 50463. Vlach Qt (+ Bagatelles)

      Artia ALPS 706

    Vanguard VMS 75004. Slovak Qt (+ Quartet No. 12)

    Columbia ML 5143. Budapest Stg Qt (+ Quartet No. 12)

    Epic LC-3490. Netherlands Qt (+ Quartet No. 12)

    London 387. Boskovsky Qt

    London/STS 15399. Gabrieli Stg Qt (+ Quartet No. 14)

    SVBX 549. Kohon Qt in "Dvořák Chamber Music" Vol. I

STRING QUARTET NO. 11 IN C MAJOR, op.61 (B.121) (1881)

   * Calliope CAL 9617. Talich Quartet (+ Quartet No. 12)

      Calliope 1617

      Calliope CAL-161799 (+ Quartet No. 12; Smetana; Janáček) (three LP)

   * Musicmasters 60102. Mendelssohn Quartet (+ Mendelssohn)

      Musicmasters 60102F

      MHS 7214

Specifically written for performers in Vienna, opus 61 observes classical propriety. Consequently, the Quartet moves in a direction entirely different from the Slavic flavor of the preceding E-flat Quartet, without too obvious homage to Beethoven or Schubert; by this date Dvořák's own developed powers and creative assurance were firmly established. This is spacious music reliably constructed, but not Dvořák in folk costume.

Supplementary Recordings:

   RCA ARL1-0082. Guarneri Qt (+ Terzetto)

   RCA LM-2524. Julliard Qt (+ Wolf)

   Supraphon DV 5750/ SV 8249 Novák Qt

   Concert Hall Society 1075. Gordon Qt

   SVBX 549. Kohon Qt In "Dvořák Chamber Music" Vol. I

   DGG 2740 117. Prague Qt (complete String Quartets)

STRING QUARTET NO. 12 IN F MAJOR, op.96 (B.179) (1893) "American"

* Denon C37-7338. Smetana Quartet (+ Quintet, op.81). Rec 1980

   Denon OW 7407

* Denon CO-72540. Smetana Quartet (+ Sextet)

* Denon C37-7234. Kocian Quartet (+ Quartet No. 13)

* Calliope CAL 9617. Talich Quartet (+ Quartet No. 11) Rec 1976

   Calliope 1617

   Calliope CAL 161799 (+ Quartet No. 11; Janáček; Smetana) (three LP)

* Supraphon C37-7910. Panocha Quartet (+ Quartet No. 10)

   Supraphon 1 11 1683 (+ Haydn; Schubert)

   Quintessence PMC-7183 (+ Haydn)

* Cadenza CAD C-872-8. Stamitz Quartet (+ Quartet No. 13)

* CBS 44920-2. Tokyo String Quartet (+ Quintet, op.81)

* ProArte CDD-237. Cleveland Quartet (+ Cypresses)

* Philips 420-803-2. Guarneri Quartet (+ Smetana). Rec 1986

* DGG 419 601-2. Hagen Quartet (+ selected Cypresses; Kodály)

     DGG 419 601-1

* Bellaphon 690-01-018. Doležal Quartet (+ Quartet No. 14)

* White Label HRC-122. Bartók Quartet (+ Debussy; Ravel)

* Arabesque Z-6558. Portland String Quartet (+ Quintet, op.77)

     Arabesque ABQ-6558

* MCA MCAD 25214. Delme Quartet (+ Brahms)

* Newport Classic NC-60033. Manhattan Quartet (+ Barber et al)

* ProArte CDD-304. Varsovia Quartet (+ Haydn)

     ProArte 132 (+ Quartet No. 7)

* Philips 420 396-2. Orlando Quartet (+ Mendelssohn)

The so-called American Quartet is the product of a summer's idyll at Spillville in northeastern Iowa. Like the "New World" Symphony, this companion quartet shows Afro-American and Indian veneer. From immediate success, the piece went on to become one of the most popular examples of string quartet writing by any composer. In the Scherzo, Dvořák added a piquant touch by encoding the chirp of a pesky scarlet tanager. Everything about the American Quartet is positive, folksy and, above all, lively. This is one of the most concise, rhythmically persuasive statements Dvořák ever issued.

Supplementary Recordings:

* RCA Gold Seal 6263-2RG. Guarneri Qt (+ Piano Quintet, op.81)

* Virgin Classics VC 7 90807-2. Endellion Qt (+ Smetana)

* Supraphon/Treasury DC-80-8. Prague Qt (+ Schubert)

     Supraphon 50816

* Philips 420 876-2. Quartetto Italiano (+ Schubert; Borodin)

* Forlane UCD 16538. Quattor Enesco (+ Enesco; Janáček)

* Philips 420 958-2. Kontra Qt (+ Quartet No. 14)

Ex Libris EL 16 878. New Zurich Qt (+ Grieg)

Vanguard VMS 75004. Slovak Qt (+ Quartet No. 10)

Opus 911 0232

Pierre Verany PV 83095/CA 682. Quatuor de Provence (+ Quartet No. 9)

Europa Klassik 114 071.0. Bethien Qt (+ Haydn)

DGG 2530994. Amadeus Qt (+ Smetana)

EMI ASD 3694. Medici Qt (+ Smetana)

* Naxos 8.550251. Moyzes Qt (+ Quartet No. 14)

* Book-of-the-Month Records BOMR 7256. Emerson Qt (+ Borodin; Smetana et al) in "The Great Romantic Quartets" (four CD)

* London/Jubilee 425 537-2. Janáček Qt (+ Quintet, op.97)

London CM 9394 (STS 15207) (+ Quartet No. 9)

Hungaroton 12577. Bartók Qt (+ Quartet No. 14)

EMI RLS-765. Hollywood Stg Qt (+ Brahms; Smetana) (three LP)

Capitol P-8307 (+ Dohnanyi)

DGG 2530 0632. Prague Qt (+ Quartet No. 14)

* DGG 429 1932 (DGG 2740 117) in complete quartets

Columbia M-32792. Budapest Stg Quartet (+ Quintet, op.97)

Columbia ML-5143 (+ Quartet No. 10)

Vox SVBX 550. Kohon Qt in "Dvořák Chamber Music" Vol I

* Novello Records NYLCD 903. Budapest St Qt (+ Schubert et al) in "The Original Budapest String Quartet" Rec 1926

Additional Recordings: Supraphon DV 5536 (Smetana); Concert Hall Society 1157 (Hungarian); Epic LC-3490 (Netherlands); Oryx EXP 30 (Arriaga); DGG 18626 (Amadeus); London LLP 4 (Griller); Turnabout 37009 (Concord); Lyrichord LL 80 (Claremont); Westminster 5199 (Curtis); Stradivari 613 (Stradivari); Decca (USA) DL-9637 (Koeckert); Gasparo GS-233 (Fine Arts); CBS MS-7144 (Julliard); Centaur 1008/09 (New World) (two LP); Musical Masterpiece Society MMS-42 (Pascal) (ten-inch LP); Da Camera 007 061 (Zagreb); Schwann 16 878 (New Zurich); Intercord 185 810 (Leonhardt) (five LP)

STRING QUARTET NO. 13 IN G MAJOR, op.106 (B.192) (1895)

* Supraphon C37-7910. Panocha Quartet (+ Quartet No. 10)

* Denon CD-7234. Kocian Quartet (+ Quartet No. 12)

   Denon OF-7116-ND (+ Quartet No. 10)

* Cadenza CAD C-872-8. Stamitz Quartet (+ Quartet No. 12)

Completed soon after Dvořák had returned home from his American sojourn, the G Major Quartet shows few residual transatlantic traits. The expansion of material has been likened to newly spread wings, carried out in terms of thematic cross-references and complex structure particularly in the end movements. The superb Adagio, on the other hand, presents an untroubled surface.

Supplementary Recordings:

   London/Jubilee 414 143-1. Gabrieli Qt (+ Waltzes)

   Teldec 641933. Alban Berg Qt

   RCA ARL1-4051 Guarneri Qt

   DGG 2530 480. Prague Qt

      DGG 2740 117 (quartets complete)

   Supraphon 50172. Vlach Qt

      Crossroads 22 16 0072

   Vox SVBX 550. Kohon Qt in "Dvořák Chamber Music" Vol III

STRING QUARTET NO. 14 IN A-FLAT MAJOR, op.105 (B. 193) (1895)

* Supraphon C-37-7565. Panocha Quartet (+ Quartet No. 12)

* Denon C37-7235. Kocian Quartet (+ Quartet No. 10)

* Cadenza CAD C 873-8. Stamitz Quartet (+ Quartet No. 10)

* Bellaphon 690-01-018. Doležal Quartet (+ Quartet No. 12)

Despite the lower opus number, Dvořák completed the A-flat Quartet after he signed finis to opus 106. So the work is his valedictory, not only as a creator of string quartets, but also as a composer of absolute music. Programmatic tone poems and opera absorbed most of Dvořák's energies during his final decade.

The A-flat Quartet conveys blissful serenity removed from the tensions of its G Major companion. Notable is the second movement (*Molto vivace*), possibly Dvořák's most beguiling scherzo since the Seventh Symphony. In both quartets Dvořák's masterful eloquence is wondrous.

Supplementary Recordings:

* Philips 420 958-2. Kontra Qt (+ Quartet No. 12)

  Centaur 1008/09. New World Qt (+ Quartets Nos. 10, 12)

  Hungaroton SLPD 12577. Bartók Qt (+ Quartet No. 12)

  Supraphon 50816. Prague Qt (+ Quartet No. 12)

  DGG 2530 632. Prague Qt (+ Quartet No. 12)

    DGG 2740 117 (quartets complete)

  Vox SVBX 550. Kohon Qt in "Dvořák Chamber Music" Vol II

  RCA LM-2887. Guarneri Qt (+ Smetana)

    RCA LSC-2887

    RCA/Victrola 1232

* Naxos 8.550251. Moyzes Qt (+ Quartet No. 12)

  Westminster XWN-18519. Barylli Qt (+ Quintet, op.81)

  London/STS 15399. Gabrieli Qt (+ Quartet No. 10)

Vox 7570. Barchet Qt

Decca (USA) 9919. Janáček Qt

CYPRESSES FOR STRING QUARTET (B.152)

TWO WALTZES FOR STRING QUARTET (B.105)

See arrangements by Dvořák.

BAGATELLES (MALIČKOSTI) FOR TWO VIOLINS, CELLO AND HARMONIUM, op.57 (B.79) (1978)

* Musicmasters MMD 60180H. Orchester der Beethovenhalle Bonn conducted by Dennis Russell Davies (in string orchestra arrangement); Liviu Casleanu (v); Michal Kurkowski (v); Christian Brunnert (vc); Dennis Russell Davies (hm) (in original quartet version) (+ Serenade, op.44)

Calliope CAL 1618. Members of Prague Chamber Orchestra, directed by Otokar Stejskal (+ Serenade, op.22)

London/STS 15438. Members of Vienna Philharmonia Quintet; Walter Planyavsky (h) (+ String Quintet, op.97)

Dvořák's set of five charming rondos draws heavily on the bank of Czech folksong and resembles further Slavonic Dances, but in slow motion. The combination of instruments may seem odd today, but harmonium and strings were fairly common as an ensemble in the days of widespread home music-making.

Supplementary Recordings:

CBS M-34515. Julliard String Quartet with Firkusny (hm) (+ Quintet, op.81)

Supraphon S-13491. Suk (v); Pavlik (v); Chuchro (vc); Hála (hm) (+ Piano Quartets; Miniatures; Gavotte) (two LP)

Supraphon 1111 3491/92

Supraphon 50463. Vlach Quartet with Kampelsheimer (hm) (+ String Quartet No. 10)

Artia ALPS 706

Vox SVBX 571. Dumka Trio in "Dvořák Chamber Music" Vol IV

PIANO QUARTET NO. 1 IN D MAJOR, op. 23 (B.53) (1875)

* Supraphon C37-7602. Josef Suk (v); Josef Kod'ousek (va); Josef Chuchro (vc); Josef Hála (p) (+ Piano Quartet, op.87)

    Supraphon 1111 3491/92 (+ Piano Quartet, op.87; Miniatures; Bagatelles; Gavotte)(two LP)

    Denon OF 7040

    ProArte PAD-161

* Hyperion CDA 66287. Domus Ensemble (+ Piano Quartet, op.87)

* Dorian 90126. Ames Piano Quartet (Piano Quartet, op.87)

* DG Records MD+GL 3233. Mozart Piano Quartet (+ Stahle)

The lesser of Dvořák's two Piano Quartets is relatively light-weight. Unconventional features are three movements, a theme and variations for the slow movement, and a hybrid finale with scherzo telescoped in. Piano writing favors a filigree pattern in the upper registers, but decorates a flow of appealing melody.

Supplementary Recordings:

    Philips 6500452. Beaux Arts Trio with Trampler (va) (+ Piano Quartet, op.87)

    CBS MG-35913. Julliard Quartet with Rudolf Firkusny (p) (+ Piano Quartet, op.87) (two LP)

    Vox SVBX 571. Dumka Trio with Gerhart (va) in "Dvořák Chamber Music" Vol. IV

PIANO QUARTET NO.2 IN E-FLAT MAJOR, op.87 (B.162) (1889)

* Supraphon C-37 7602. Josef Suk (v); Josef Kod'ousek (va); Josef Chuchro (vc); Josef Hála (p) (+ Piano Quartet, op.23)

    Supraphon 1111 3491/92 (two LP)

* Bellaphon 690-01-032. Alvarez Piano Quartet with Carmen Piazzini (p) (+ Turina)

* Hyperion CDA 66287. Domus Ensemble (+ Piano Quartet, op.23)

* RCA 6256-2-RC. Members of Guarneri Quartet with Artur Rubinstein (p) (+ Faure)

   RCA LSC-3340

* Dorian 90126. Ames Piano Quartet (+ Piano Quartet No. 1)

Unaccountably, the heroic E-flat Major Piano Quartet has been overshadowed by more popular examples of the Czech master's chamber music. But under the fingers of a deeply committed collaborating pianist -- Rubinstein on RCA is surely one of these -- this sinewy, dramatic piece takes on major dimensions, particularly in the full-blooded end movements. The work sounds more complex and taxing than usual for Dvořák, but melodic fertility runs high and development strenuous. Despite a diversity of moods and material, coherence and confident stride never come into question.

Supplementary Recordings:

   CBS MG 35913. Julliard Qt with Firkusny (p) (+ Piano Quartet, op.23) (two LP)

   Rizzoli 2002. Lydian Trio with Monacelli (p) (+ Fauré)

   Stradivari 619. Galimir Qt with Jahoda (p) (+ Janáček)

   Concert Hall Society D2. Rybar (v); Kromer (v); Tusa (vc); Balsam (p)

Trios:

Integrated Sets (ops. 21; 26; 65; 90):

* Denon CO-1409/ 1410. Suk Trio (two CD)

   Supraphon 1411 2621/23 (three LP)

   MHS 3732 Z. Concordia Trio (three LP)

   Philips 6703 015. Beaux Art Trio (three LP)

   CRD 1086/88. Cohen Trio (+ Romantic Pieces; Rondo) (three LP)

* Le Chant du Monde LDC 2781045/46. Trio de Prague (two CD)

PIANO TRIO NO. 1 IN B-FLAT Major, op.21 (B.51) (1875)

* Newport Classic 60074-2. Raphael Trio (+ Trio, op.26)

* Teldec 8.44198. Trio Fontenay (+ Brahms)

* Denon CO-1409. Suk Trio (+ Trio, op.26)

   Denon OX-7114-ND (+ Trio, op.26)

* London 421 118-2. Chung Trio (+ Trio, op.65)

This sprightly opus amply demonstrates that by age 34 Dvořák had his distinctive feel for chamber music well in hand. The revision process doubtless meant improvement, but there is some reason to believe that Dvořák had written prior pieces in this medium, later destroyed.

Supplementary Recordings:

   Panton 8111 0564. Ars Trio (+ Martinů)

   Vox SVBX 571. Dumka Trio in "Dvořák Chamber Music" Vol. IV

   Pearl SHE 553. Beaux Arts Trio (+ Mendelssohn)

PIANO TRIO NO. 2 IN G. MINOR, op.26 (B.56) (1876)

* Newport Classic NCD-60074-2. Raphael Trio (+ Trio, op.21)

* Denon CO-1409. Suk Trio (+ Trio, op.21)

* Preciosa/Aulos 66008. Dvořák Trio (+ Trio, op.65)

* Intercord/Saphir 830.863. Odeon Trio (+ Quintet, op.81)

The note of seriousness, compared to the more extroverted First Piano Trio, coincides with the loss of an infant daughter. Even the Scherzo seems relatively joyless.

Supplementary Recordings:

ProArte PAD 130. Odeon Trio (+ Trio, op.90)

CRD 1086. Cohen Trio (+ Trio, op.21)

Westminster W- 9024. Fournier (v); Janigro (vc); Badura-Skoda (p) (+ Trio, op.90)

Vox SVBX 588. Dumka Trio in "Dvorak Chamber Music" Vol. V

PIANO TRIO NO. 3 IN F MINOR, op. 65 (B.130) (1883)

* CBS MK 44527. Young Uck Kim (v); Yo-Yo Ma (vc); Emanuel Ax (p) (+ Trio, op.90)

* Chandos CHAN 8320. Borodin Trio

    Chandos ABRD 1107

* Denon CO-1410. Suk Trio (+ Trio, op.90)

* Preciosa/Aulos 66008. Dvořák Trio (+ Trio, op.26)

* Intercord/Saphir INT 830.849. Odeon Trio (+ Trio, op.90)

    Nonesuch H-71397. Raphael Trio

    Sonar SD 180

* London 421 118-2. Chung Trio (+ Trio, op.21)

Like the Seventh Symphony, the F Minor Trio comes from the dark night of Dvořák's soul, when he wrestled with friendly pressures to move to Vienna. Struggle absorbs all four movemnts to varying degree, with climax in the poignant, centrally placed *Poco adagio*. The trio sweeps on to a breathless conclusion; Dvořák's stubborn resolve and Czech sympathies clearly have won through. Among piano trios, this work stands as a giant.

Supplementary Recordings:

Supraphon 50817. Suk Trio

    Quintessence PMC-7204

Denon OX 7122. Suk Trio

Columbia M-33447. Heifetz (v); Piatigorsky (vc); Pennario (p) (+ Stravinsky; Gliere; Handel-Halvorsen)

TR Records TRC-101. Mirecourt Trio

Laurel Record LR-127. Western Arts Trio (+ Debussy)

Gallo 30-424. Trio Musiviva (+ Martin)

DGG 253037. Yuval Trio

Concert Hall Society CHS 1117. Kaufman (v); Cervera (vc); Balsam (p)

Westminster XWN 18176. Oistrakh (v); Krushevitsky (vc); Oborin (p) (+ Smetana)

Monitor S-2071. Oistrakh Trio (+ Haydn)

Vox SVBX 588. Dumka Trio in "Dvořák Chamber Music" Vol. V

CRD 1088. Cohen Trio (+ Romantic Pieces; Rondo)

PIANO TRIO NO. 4 IN E. MINOR, op.90 (B. 166) (1891), "Dumky"

* CBS MK 44527. Young Uck Kim (v); Yo-Yo Ma (vc); Emanuel Ax (p) (+ Trio, op.65)

* Chandos CHAN 9445. Borodin Trio (+ Smetana)

    Chandos ABRD 1107

* Virgin Classics VC 7 90736-2. Nash Ensemble with Jan Brown (p) (+ Quintet, op.81)

* Denon C37-7057. Suk Trio (+ Suk)

* Philips 416 297-2. Beaux Arts Trio (+ Mendelssohn)

* Intercord/ Saphir INT 831.849. Odeon Trio (+ Trio, op.65)

* Supraphon/ Suk Treasury 11 0704-2 111. Suk Trio (+ Smetana)

Dvořák seems to have been first to slip the Ukranian dumka into serious composition, and the term has caused confusion ever since. The dumka (plural in Czech dumky) is not a folk dance, rather a sung lament with alternating mournful and animated sections. The bivalent character of the dumka lies close to his own artistic temperament, and out of this he derived a fresh principle of form.

Dvořák employed the <u>dumka</u> in several compositions, but the Trio No. 4 stands as the prime example. Each of six movements consists of a stylized <u>dumka</u> in which a melancholic mood suddenly becomes dispelled by more cheerful signals at faster tempo. The first three <u>dumky</u> play as an unbroken chain; the remaining three stand as separate movements. Dvořák's lyric fund gives most generously in this celebrated chamber composition.

<u>Supplementary Recordings</u>:

* Lyrinx CYR CD 028. Trio Gabriel Fauré (+ Suk)

   Lyrinx 8111-028 (+ Suk)

* Musicmasters 60152/53. Swensen (v); Brey (vc); Kahane (p) (+ Mozart et al) in live performance at the 1986 Spoletto Festival (Two CD)

* Smithsonian Collection ND-034. Castle Trio (+ Smetana)

   Turnabout TV 34074. Dumka Trio (+ Quintet, op.81)

      Vox SVBX 571 in "Dvorak Chamber Music" Vol. IV

   Vox PLP 2070. Trio de Trieste

   Wilson Audiophile W 8416. Francesca Trio

      * WCD-8416

   Westminster W-9024. Fournier (v); Janigro (vc); Badura-Skoda (p)

   Westminster XWN 18175. D. Oistrakh (v); Knushevitzky (vc); Oborin (p) (+ Smetana)

      Monitor MCS 2070E

   Supraphon DM 5037. Czech Trio

   ProArte PAD-130. Odeon Trio (+ Trio, op.26)

   Stradivari 620. Ricci (v); Eidus (vc); Mittman (p) (+ Smetana)

   CRD 1087. Cohen Trio

   Marlboro MRS-13. Phillips (v); Grossman(vc); Canino (p) (+ Boccherini)

   Supraphon 1111 1089. Czech Trio (+ Novák)

   Panton 01 1234. Smetana Trio (+ Suk)

Denon OX-7134. Suk Trio (+ Suk)

RCA LSC-3068. Heifetz (v); Piatigorsky (vc); Lateiner (p) (+ Spohr)

DGG 2930594. Yuval Trio (+ Smetana)

HMV HQS 1239. Members of Drolc Quartet with Crowson (p) (+ Terzetto)

String Trios:

TERZETTO IN C MAJOR FOR TWO VIOLINS AND VIOLA, op.74 (B.148) (1887)

* Supraphon CO-2254. Members of Panocha Quartet (+ Serenade, op.44)

* Unicorn-Kanchana DKP (CD) 9079. The English String Quartet (+ Cypresses)

Originally intended for amateur string players, Terzetto may seem like a top-heavy string quartet yet it works. Melodic allure alone makes the piece a delight. Further attractions include a snappy scherzo and an excellent set of variations by way of finale.

Supplementary Recordings:

* Dynamic CDS-45. Accardo (v) and colleagues (+ Quintet, op.77)

Supraphon DM 5542. Members of Vlach Qt (+ Hlobil)

RCA ARL1-0082. Members of Guarneri Qt (+ Quartet, op.61)

HNH Records 4069. Members of New London Quintet (+ Suk)

Classic Editions 1033. Classic Trio (+ Kodály)

HMV HQS 1239. Members of Drolc Qt (+ Trio, op.90)

Musica Viva MV 30-1073. Japan String Trio (+ Dohnányi)

Chant du Monde LDX 78786. Pikaizen (v); Rusin (v); I. Oistrakh (va) (+ Piano Quintet, op. 81)

MINIATURES (DROBNOSTI) FOR TWO VIOLINS AND VIOLA, op.75a (B.149) (1887)

Supraphon 1111 3491/92 (S-13491; 10 3491-1 132. Joseph Suk (v) and associates (+ Piano Quartets; Bagatelles; Gavotte) (two LP)

Supraphon 50824. Members of Dvorak Quartet (+ Sextet)

When his friends found Terzetto too difficult for their capacities, Dvořák tried again. The resultant string trio was named Miniatures when finally published in 1948. Meanwhile, the same music had become famous in the composer's recasting for violin and piano (see Four Romantic Pieces).

Supplementary Recordings:

Campion Records RRCD 1301. Camerata Nova (+ Sonatina; Five Dances; Rusalka "Song to the Moon). Arr string orchestra

GAVOTTE FOR THREE VIOLINS (B.164) (1890)

Supraphon 1111 3491 (S-13491-1 132). Josef Suk (v) and associates (+ Piano Quartets; Bagatelles; Miniatures) (two LP)

Among less familiar Dvořák items is this modest dance for violin ensemble, a piece intended for less than professional executants.

Solo Instrument and Piano:

Integrated Sets

* Supraphon/Suk Treasury 11-0703-2.   Josef Suk (v); Alfred Holeček (p).
  Sonata in F Major; <u>Sonatina in G Major</u>; <u>Four Romantic Pieces</u>; <u>Ballad in D
  Major</u>; <u>Mazurek</u>; <u>Slavonic Dance</u> op.46 no.2; <u>Humoresque</u>. "Antonín Dvořák:
  Compositions for Violin and Piano"

  Supraphon/Master Series MS 111 1311/12 (two LP)

  Telefunken 6.42038.   Klaus Storck (vc); Karl Engel (p).   <u>Rondo in G Minor</u>;
  <u>Silent Woods</u>; <u>Polonaise in A Major</u>; <u>Slavonic Dances</u> op.46 nos. 3, 8
  (+ Janacek) in Samtliche Werke fur Violoncello und Klavier"

SONATA IN F MAJOR FOR VIOLIN AND PIANO, op.56 (B.106) (1880)

* Supraphon/Suk Treasury 11-0703-2.   Josef Suk (v); Alfred Holeček (p) in
  "Compositions for Violin and Piano"

  Supraphon MS 111 1311/12 (two LP)

Composed between revisions of the Violin Concerto, the F-Major Sonata received
the approval of the eminent Joseph Joachim.   Yet the violin community as a whole
does not seem to have become overly enraptured by the piece, judging by relatively
few recordings.   Each of the three movements exhibits aspects of variation technique
with departures from strict classical contrasts.   The opening *Allegro ma non troppo*,
like the following *Poco sostenuto*, gives off the aroma of Brahms; serious, sometimes
intimate matters lie under discussion.   The light-hearted *Allegro molto*, the most
immediately attractive movement, is more recognizably Dvořák.

Supplementary Recordings:

Orion 7020.   Temianka (v); Robbins (p) (+ Sonatina; <u>Romantic Pieces</u>)

Westminster XWN 18066.   Rybar (v); Holetschek (p) (+ Quintet, op.77;
<u>Romantic Pieces</u>)

MHS 3415.   Naegele (v); Krieger (p) (+ Sonatina; <u>Romantic Pieces</u>)

Supraphon DV 5515 (10023).   Suk (v); Panenka (p) (+ Sonatina)

SONATINA IN G MAJOR FOR VIOLIN AND PIANO, op.100 (B.183) (1893)

* Supraphon/Suk Treasury 11-0703-2. Josef Suk (v); Alfred Holeček (p) in "Compositions for Violin and Piano"

   Supraphon MS 1 11 1311/12

* EMI CDC 7 47399-2 (Angel CDC-47399). Itzhak Perlman (v); Samuel Sanders (p) (+ Romantic Pieces; Smetana)

   Angel DS-38134

   When still living in New York, Dvořák reached his opus 100 which he dedicatd to other opus numbers, namely his six children. Genial and warm-hearted, with touches of Indianism and whiffs of Moravian folksong, the Sonatina has become deservedly popular. The beguiling Larghetto uses a melody which Dvořák reputedly jotted down while gazing at Minnehaha Falls in Minnesota. Subsequent arrangers have given names like "Indian Lament," "Indian Lullaby" and "Indian Canzonetta" to this movement, none of which stem from the composer.

Supplementary Recordings:

   Klavier KS-503. Zsigmondy (v); Nissen (p) (+ Prokofiev et al) in "The Virtuoso Violin"

   Orion 7020. Temianka (v); Robbins (p) (+ Sonata; Romantic Pieces)

   Nocturne (Germany) SM 1051. Mannheimer Kammerduo (+ Smetana et al)

   Supraphon 1111 2970. Matousek (v); Adamec (p) (+ Smetana; Suk)

   MHS 3415. Naegele (v); Krieger (p) (+ Sonata; Romantic Pieces)

      Da Camera 93 308

   MHS 7206. Philipo (v); Abramovic (p) (+ Romance; Mazurek; Romantic Pieces)

   Swedish Society Discophile SLT 33228. Wickström (v); Bartov (p)

   Melodya 43305. Prihoda (v); ? (p) (+ Hubay)

Also see arrangements for Flute and Piano and Dvořák-Kriesler Indian Lament.

(FOUR) ROMANTIC PIECES, op.75 (B.150) (1887)

* Angel CDC-47399 (EMI CDC 7 47399-2). Itzhak Perlman (v); Samuel Sanders (p) (+ Sonatina; Smetana)

 Nonesuch 71350. Sergiu Luca (v); Paul Schoenfeld (p) (+ Janacek; Smetana)

 CBS M-39114. Isaac Stern (v); Alexander Zakin (p) (+ Brahms; Enesco; Schumann)

* Philips 416 158-2. Pinchas Zukerman (v); Marc Neikrug (p) (+ De Falla et al) in "Salut d'amour"

The popular Romantic Pieces, four gem-like mood pictures, are a recasting of the string trio posthumously published as Miniatures (op.75a), originally intended as a companion to the Terzetto.

Supplementary Recordings:

 Sheffield Lab 18. Steinhardt (v); Mayorga (p) (+ R. Strauss)

 Capitol 7506. Kaufman (v); Balsam (p) (+ Schumann) (ten-inch LP)

 Masters of the Bow MB 1041 (+ Saint-Saens et al) in "The Romantic Violin"

 RBM Best. Nr. 3059. Boettcher (v); Trede-Boettcher (p) (+ Ravel; de Falla; Bartók)

 Supraphon 111 1311/12. Suk (v); Holeček (p) in "Compositions for Violin and Piano"

 * Supraphon/Suk Treasury 110 703-2

 MHS 3415. Naegele (v); Krieger (p) (+ Sonata; Sonatina)

 Da Camera 93 308

 MHS 7206. Philipo (v); Abramovic (p) (+ Sonatina; Romance; Mazurek)

 RCA (Italy) RL 31462. Ughi (v); ? (p) (+ Paganini et al)

 Westminster 5015. Rybar (v); Holetschek (p) (+ Sonata)

 Westminster XWN 18066 (+ Quintet, op.77)

 Orion 7020. Temianka (v); Robbins (p) (+ Sonata; Sonatina)

Klavier KS-503. Zsigmondy (v); Nissen (p) (+ Sonatina; Prokofiev et al) in "The Virtuoso Violin"

* Dynamic DC UO1. Gulli (v); Cavallo (p) (+ Corelli et al)

* Dynamic CDS-81. Accardo (v); Canino (p) (+ Quintet, op.81)

ROMANCE IN F MINOR FOR VIOLIN AND PIANO, op.11 (B.38) (c 1873)

MHS 7206. Daniel Philipo (v); Charles Abramovic (p) (Sonatina; Romantic Pieces; Mazurek)

NOTTURNO IN B MAJOR FOR VIOLIN AND PIANO, op.40 (B.48) (c 1875) (arr from B.19)

Supraphon MS 111 1311/12. Josef Suk (v); Alfred Holeček (p) in "Compositions for Violin and Piano"

MAZUREK FOR VIOLIN AND PIANO, op.49 (B.89) (1879)

Supraphon MS 1311/12. Josef Suk (v); Alfred Holeček (p) in "Compositions for Violin and Piano"

MHS 7206. Daniel Philipo (v); Charles Abramovic (p) (+ Sonatina; Romance; Romantic Pieces)

Note: For Notturno also see works for orchestra; for Romance and Mazurek also see works for solo instrument and orchestra.

BALLADE IN D MINOR FOR VIOLIN AND PIANO, op.15/I (B.139) (1884)

Supraphon MS 111 1311/12. Josef Suk (v); Alfred Holeček (p) in "Compositions for Violin and Piano"

This modest, obscure Dvořák piece may derive from an unused sketch for the Seventh Symphony.

SILENT WOODS FOR CELLO AND PIANO, op.68, No. 5 (B.173)

Supraphon 1 11 2179. Josef Suk (va); Jan Panenka (p) (+ Quintet, op.97)

Calliope 1676. André Navarra (vc); Erika Kilcher (p) (+ Humoresque; Rondo; de Falla et al)

When cellists are moved to record <u>Silent Woods</u> (Waldesruhe) they usually prefer the composer's version with orchestral accompaniment. Josef Suk's viola transcription provides another alternative.

<u>Supplementary Recordings:</u>

> Telefunken 6.42038. Klaus Storck (vc); Karl Engel (p) (+ <u>Rondo</u>; <u>Polonaise;</u> Janáček) in "Samtliche Werke für Violoncello und Klavier"

POLONAISE IN A MINOR FOR CELLO AND PIANO (B.94) (1879)

* Philips 412 373-2. Heinrich Schiff (vc); Elizabeth Leonskaja (p) (+ Rachmaninoff; Sibelius)

  Telefunken 6.42038. Klaus Storck (vc); Karl Engel (p) in "Samtliche Werke für Violoncello and Klavier" (+ Janacek)

  Orion 7287. King (vc); Leviev (p) (+ Reger et al)

* Cybella CY 8007. Celia Tsan (vc); Jean-Louis Haguenauer (p) (+ Mendelssohn et al) in "Onze pieces pour violoncelle et piano"

Also see works for solo instrument and orchestra.

RONDO IN G MINOR FOR CELLO AND PIANO, op.94 (B.181) (1891)

* Kontrapunkt 32103. Michaela Fukačová (vc); Ivan Klansky (p) (+ Franck et al)

* Duraphon HD 423. Martin Schucan (vc); Hansjorg Fink (p) (+ Liszt et al)

* RBM CD 63112. Wolfgang Boettcher (vc); Ursula Trede-Boettcher (p) (+ Popper et al) in "Perles musicales"

  CRD 1088. Robert Cohen (vc); Rael (p) (+ <u>Romantic Pieces</u>; Trio, op.65)

  > CRD 1086/88

  Calliope 1676. André Navarra (vc); Erika Kilcher (p) (+ <u>Silent Woods</u>; <u>Humoresque</u>; "Songs my mother..."; Faure et al)

  Orion 73103 Mihaly Virizlay (vc); Penneys (p) (+ recital)

  Crystal Records S-303. Lustgarten (vc); Newman (p) (+ Bach et al)

Telefunken 6.42038. Klaus Storck (vc); Karl Engel (p) in "Samtliche Werke für Violoncello und Klavier" (+ Janacek)

Thorofon MTH 266. Rainer Hochmuth (v); Horst Gobel (p) (+ Paganini et al) in "Salut d' amour"

V

Keyboard Works

Documentation of Dvořák's solo piano music has been assisted enormously in an integral edition recorded in stereo by Radoslav Kvapil. All six LPs come boxed as Supraphon 1111 2131/6.

Supraphon 1 11 0820:

Silhouettes, op.8; Waltzes, op.54

Supraphon 1 11 0566:

Poetic Tone Pictures, op.85

Supraphon 1 11 0865:

Suite in A Major, op.98; Humoresques, op.101

* Supraphonet 11 1113-2 (+ Piano Concerto). *Humoresques only*

Supraphon 1 11 1395:

Ecologues, op.56; Album Leaves; Piano Pieces, op.52; Impromptu in G Major

Supraphon 1 11 1179:

Mazurkas, op.56. Note: The Mazurkas and Ecologues share an identical opus number.

Dumka, op.12/1; Furiant, op.12/2; Impromptu in D Minor

Humoresque in F sharp Major

Lullaby (Berceuse)

Capriccio (Allegretto scherzando)

Supraphon 1 11 0682:

Tema con variazioni, op.36

Two Furiants, op.42

Dumka, op.35

Two Minuets, op.28

Scottish Dances, op.41

Supplementary Recordings:

TEMA CON VARIAZIONI IN A FLAT MAJOR, op.36 (B.65) (1876)

Candide CE 31064. Rudolf Firkusny (+ Poetic Tone Pictures; Silhouettes)

* Arabesque Z-6532. Gena Raps (+ Waltzes). Rec 1984

Arabesque 6532

Supraphon SUA ST 50525. Rumjana Atanasova (+ Schumann; Smetana) in "Laureates of the International Competition" Prague Spring 1963

Supraphon LPV 109. Josef Páleniček (+ Symphonic Variations)

SIHOUETTES, op.8 (B.98) (1879)

Candide CE 31067. Rudolf Firkusny (+ Poetic Pictures; Tema con variazioni)

WALTZES, op.54 (B.101) (1880)

* Arabesque Z-6532. Gena Raps (+ Tema con variazioni)

Arabesque 6532

Baroque Records 2873. Marie-Aimee Varro + Mazurkas; Schumann; Liszt). Nos. 2, 4, 5 only

Waltzes No. 1 in A and No. 4 in D also exist in a version for string quartet arranged by Dvořák. Orchestral arrangements have been prepared by others (see arrangements).

MAZURKAS, op.56 (B.111) (1880)

Candide CE 31070. Rudolf Firkusny (+ Humoresques)

Baroque Records 2873. Marie-Aimee Varro. Nos. 2, 3, 6 only

POETIC TONE PICTURES, op. 85 (B. 161) (1889)

Genesis GS 1019. Gerald Robbins

Candide 31067. Rudolf Firkusny. Nos. 3, 6, 9 only

SUITE IN A MAJOR, op.98 (B.184) (1894)

Genesis 1025. Radoslav Kvapil (+ Humoresques)

This was the fifth work Dvořák composed during his residence in the United States. A year later he recast the piece for large orchestra which has come to be known as the American Suite.

HUMORESQUES, op.101 (B. 187) (1894)

* Vox Prima MWCD-7114. Rudolf Firkusny (+ Piano Concerto)

Candide CE 31070 (+ Mazurkas)

Genesis GS 1025. Radoslav Kvapil (+ Suite in A)

Supraphon 1011 3918. Jan Herman (+ Impromptu in D Minor; Dumka, op.12/1; Suk; Smetana; Novák). Nos 1 and 7 only

Of the eight Humoresques in op.101, the seventh in G flat Major has become one of the most widely-known piano pieces ever written. Much of its fame, however, has come in the form of myriad arrangements, especially one for violin and piano by Fritz Kreisler.

Humoresque No. 7 (original version for solo piano):

* EMI/Laser CDZ 762523. Moura Lympany

* Naxos/Enigma 7 74611-2. Balazs Szokoloy

* CBS CD CBS 44728. Leonard Pennario

* LaserLite 15 603. Jeno Jando

* CBS MLK 45628. Philippe Entremont in "Greatest Hits: The Piano"

   CBS Classics 61294

* London/Weekend Classics 417 884-2. Joseph Cooper in "Liebestraum"

* Kingdom KCLCD 2002. Christopher Headington in "Pictures and Pleasures"

* AVM Classics AVMCD 1005. Richard Tilling in "Music in Miniature"
  Vol I

   Europa/Klassik 114 068.0. Jorg Demus

Piano Collection:

* Dorian DOR 90121. Waltz, op.54/l; "Old Castle" from op.55; Silhouettes, op.8/12. Antonin Kubalek (p) in "Czech Miniature Masterpieces"

PRELUDE AND FUGHETTA IN D MAJOR (B.302) (1859)

   Christophorus-Verlag SCGLX 73819.   Helmut P. Tramnitz (o) in "Orgelromantik in Europa"

Piano Duets:

SLAVONIC DANCES, op.46 (B.78) (1878)

SLAVONIC DANCES, op.72 (B.145) (1886)

* Arabesque Z-6559. Artur Balsam and Gena Raps. Complete

   Arabesque ABQ 6559

* Price-Less D 14163. Francis Veri and Michael Jamanis. Complete

118 Keyboard Works

- * Opus 9351 1960. Peter Toperczer and Marián Lapšanský. Complete

    Opus 3311 1864/65

- * Hyperion CDA 66204. Peter Noke and Helen Krizos. Complete

- * Olympia OCD 362. Thorson and Thurber. Complete in "Complete Works for Piano Duet, Vol I"

    DGG 2531 349. Alfons and Aloys Kontarsky. Complete

    Turnabout TV 4060. Alfred Brendel and Walter Klein. Complete

    Vox STPL 511.620

    Supraphon 1 11 1301/02. Vlastimil Lejsek and Věra Lejsková (+ Legends 1-4). Complete

    Connoisseur Society CSQ 2146. Michel Beroff and Jean-Phillipe Collard. Complete

- * Music and Arts Programs of America CD-623. Moon and Lee (+ Smetana; Martinů). Opus 72 only

- * MCA MCAD 25891. John Ogden and Brenda Lewis (+ Milhaud et al). Opus 46, Nos. 1, 2, 3 only

LEGENDS, op.59 (B.117) (1881)

- * Price-Less D 22646. Frances Veri and Michael Jamanis (+ From the Bohemian Forest)

- * Arion ARN 68014. Christian Ivaldi and Noel Lee (+ From the Bohemian Forest)

- * Etcetera KTC-1032. Wyneke Jordans and Leo Van Doeselaar

    Etcetera ETC-1032

Also see Works for Orchestra.

FROM THE BOHEMIAN FOREST (ZE ŠUMAVY), op.68 (B.133) (1884)

* Price-Less D 22646. Frances Veri and Michael Jamanis (duo p) (+ <u>Legends</u>)

* Arion ARN 68014. Christian Ivaldi and Noel Lee (duo p) (+ <u>Legends</u>)

Long unavailable on records in complete form, this suite of six character pieces runs a gamut of romantic moods and images: "In the Spinning Room," "By the Black Lake," "Walpurgis Night," "In wait," "Silent Woods," "In stormy times." The fifth number, "Silent Woods," has long led an independent existence in the cellist's repertoire as arranged for cello and piano (later orchestrated) by the composer.

VI

Song Cycles, Solo Songs, Duets

CYPRESSES (CYPŘIŠE) (B.11) (1865). Eighteen songs on poems by Gustav Pfleger-Moravský

Recordings of the original song cycle do not seem extant. Revised selections have been published as Four Songs, op.2, and Love Songs, op.83. Dvorak further arranged Cypresses in twelve settings for string quartet.

FOUR SONGS, op.2 (B. 124) (1882)

> Etcetera ETC-1007. Carolyn Watkinson (s); Tan Crone (p) (+ Berg; Bizet et al)

LOVE SONGS, op.83 (B.160) (1888)

> Orfeo S-066831. Edita Gruberová (s); Erik Werba (p) (+ Brahms; R. Strauss) (Cz)

* Capriccio 10053. Peter Schreier (t); Marián Lapšanský (p) (+ Gypsy Songs; Biblical Songs (G)

> Spectrum SR-193. John Ostendorf (b-ba); Rudolph Palmer (p) (+ Serbian Songs; Folk Tunes; Four Songs; Children's Song) in "The Unknown Dvorak"

Supplementary Recordings:

> Supraphon 1 12 1349. Jindrak (ba); Holeček (p) in "Cycles of Songs"

> Supraphon 1112 3348. Blachut (t); Pohlreich (p) in "Beno Blachut Song Recital"

> Westminster XWN 18516 (WL 5324). Roessel-Majdan (c); Holetschek (p) (+ Biblical Songs; Gypsy Songs)

FIVE SONGS TO POEMS BY ELIŠKA KRÁSNOHORSKÁ, (B.23) (1871)

> Supraphon 1112 3348. Beno Blachut (t); Ferdinand Pohlreich (p). "Obstacles" ("Překážky") only

TWO BALLADS FROM KAREL JAROMÍR ERBEN, op.5 (B.24; 24a) (1871)

> Supraphon 1112 3348. Beno Blachut (t); Ferdinand Pohlreich (p). No. 2 "Rosemarine" ("Rozmaryna") only

FOUR SERBIAN FOLK POEMS, op.6 (B.29) (1872)

> Spectrum SR-193. John Ostendorf (bs-b); Katherine Ciesinski (mz-s); Rudolph Palmer (p) (Cz and G)

SONGS FROM THE DVUR KRALOVE MANUSCRIPT op.7 (B.30) (1872)

> No recording known.

FOUR SONGS, op.82 (B.157) (1883). Czech poems in German translation by Otilie Malybrok-Stieler

> Spectrum SR-193. Katherine Ciesinski (mz-s); Rudolph Palmer (p) (G).

EVENING SONGS (VEČERNÍ PÍSNĚ), opp.3, 9, 31 (B.61) (1876). Twelve songs on poems by Vitězslav Hálek

> Supraphon 1112 3348. Beno Blachut (t); Ferdinand Pohlreich (p)
>
> > Nos. 1-4 (op.3)
> >
> > Nos. 3 and 4 (op.9)

THREE MODERN GREEK SONGS (TŘI NOVOŘECKÉ BÁSNĚ), op.50 (B.84) (1878)

> Three Greek national songs translated into Czech by Václav Bolemír Nebeský.
>
> Supraphon 1 12 1349. Jindřich Jindrák (b); Alfred Holeček (p)

IN FOLK TONE (V NARODNIM TONU), op.73 (B.146) (1886). From Slovak and Czech folk poetry

> Acanta/Bellaphon 680.23.330. Lucia Popp (s); Geoffrey Parsons (p) (+ Prokofiev; Kodály; Janáček)
>
> Meridian E 77042. Sarah Walker (mz-s); Roger Vignoles (p) (+ Gypsy Songs; Brahms)

Spectrum SR-193. Grayson Hirst (t); Rudolph Palmer (p)

GYPSY SONGS (ZIGEUNERMELODIEN; CIGÁNSKÉ MELODIE), op.55 (B.104) (1880).

Seven poems by Adolph Heyduk.

* Capriccio 10053. Peter Schreier (t); Marián Lapšanský (p) (G)

* Simax PSC-1019. Edith Thallaug (mz-s); Eva Knardahl (p) (+ Falla; Ravel; Montsalvatge) (G)

Nonesuch 79060-1. Lucy Shelton (s); Lambert Orkis (p) (+ Liszt; Wolf et al) (Cz) Rec 1983

Meridian E 77042. Sarah Walker (mz-s); Roger Vignoles (p) (Cz)

Supplementary Recordings:

Supraphon 1 12 1349. Jindřich Jindrák (b); Alfred Holeček (p)

Telefunken/Aspekte 642214. Peter Schreier (t); Rudolf Dunkel (p)

Everest 3247. Maureen Forrester (c); John Newmark (p). Note: Title is misidentified as "Seven Bohemian Songs" both on the sleeve and label.

Intercord 185.810. Julia Hamari (a); Herbert Giesen (p) (+ Symphony No. 9; Serenade, op.22 etc) (five LP)

Electrola C 063-29 085. Brigitte Fassbaender (mz-s); Karl Engel (p)

Vanguard VRS 446. Anny Felbermeyer (s); Victor Graef (p)

Westminster WL 5324. Hildegard Roessel-Majdan (c); Franz Holetschek (p)

Gypsy Song No. 4: "Songs my mother taught me," "Als die alte Mutter;" "Kdyz mne stara matka zpívat ucivala"

This is one of the best-known of all art songs; recordings as a separate item are legion.

Supraphon 50890. Vera Soukupová (Cz)

Telefunken 6.42683 AH. Mirella Freni (G)

Angel 36296. Victoria de los Angeles (G)

Angel S-35383. Elizabeth Schwarzkopf (E)

Decca SPA 578. Joan Sutherland (E)

RCA LSC-3967. Hanne-Lore Kuhse (G)

CBS M 36682. Elly Ameling

Supraphon DM 5235. Marta Krasová (Cz)

* Pearl/ GEMM CD 9353. Nellie Melba. (Stated to have been recorded in 1913. HMV DB 362, matrix no. A13907)

* EMI CDM 7 69502-2. Victoria de Los Angeles

* Cantabile BIM 701-2. Rosa Ponselle (two CD)

Stanford Archive of Recorded Sound StARS 1000. Nellie Melba (s); Frank St. Leger (p). Rec 1916. Note: Sung transposed to D flat.

RCA/Camden CAL 325. Jeannette MacDonald (E)

BIBLICAL SONGS (BIBLICKÉ PÍSNĚ), op.99 (B.185) (1894). Text: Psalms of King David from the 16th-century Bible of Králice

* Chandos CHAN 8608. Brian Rayner Cook (b); Scottish National Orchestra conducted by Neeme Järvi (+ Symphony No. 4) (Cz) Rec 1987

* Capriccio 10053. Peter Schreier (t); Marián Lapšanský (p) (+ Love Songs; Gypsy Songs) (G) Rec 1983

* Big Ben Phonogram 861-006. Birgit Finnila (c); Malmo Symphony Orchestra conducted by Vernon Handley (+ Ferstrom) (Cz) Rec 1987

These ten settings from one of the core documents of Czech Protestantism present Dvořák's own trust in the Lord in an open, pure and direct manner.   They sound particularly resonant with orchestral accompaniment which Dvořák himself supplied to the first five songs in the set.

Supplementary Recordings:

Supraphon 50898. Věra Soukupová (c); Ivan Moravec (p) (Cz)

Westminster 18516. Hilde Roessel-Majdan (c); Franz Holetschek (p) (G)

Music Library Recording MLR 7024. Esther Lucrecia Duarte (c); Frieda Ann Murphy (p) (E)

Supraphon/Master Series MS 0981-2. Jindřich Jindrák (b); Prague SO/ Smetacek. Nos. 1-5 only

DGG 138644. Dietrich Fischer-Dieskau (b); Jörg Demus (p). Nos. 1-6 only

     Heliodor HS 25082

Oryx/ Romantic 1829. Ulf Nordquist (b); Ralph Davier (p) (+ Brahms). Selections

Supraphon 11 0061-1 211. Vilém Přibyl (t); Milan Masa (p) (+ Smetana; Beethoven)

Preciosa/Aulos PRE 68 518 AVL. Peter Zeithen (b); Gorda Zeithen-Hantich (p) (+ Mussorgsky)

MORAVIAN DUETS. Twenty-three duets based on Moravian folk poems (1875-77; 1881):

Opus 20 (B.50). Four duets for soprano, tenor and piano

Opus 29 (B.60). Five duets for soprano, alto and piano

Opus 32 (B.62). Nine duets for soprano, alto and piano

Opus 38 (B.69). Four duets for soprano, alto and piano

No opus no. (B.118). One duet for soprano and contralto with piano, "There on our roof" ("Na tej nasej střeše")

Supraphon 1112 1110. Eva Zikmundová (s); Ivo Žídek (t); Věra Soukupová (a); Alfred Holeček (p). Complete set

Composed in spurts, the <u>Moravian Duets</u> all derive from <u>Moravian National Songs</u> compiled by František Sušil (first edition 1835), but the melodies are Dvořák's own. These vocal gems drew the attention of Brahms, among others, and did much to start Dvořák on his path to international fame. Performing these fresh, tuneful duets with chorus seems of questionable merit.

<u>Supplementary Recordings</u>:

* Supraphon CD 72646. Kühn Mixed Chorus/ Pavel Kühn; Stanislav Bogunia (p). Opp. 20; 38; 32; "There on our roof"

   Supraphon 1112 4093

   Columbia MS 6936. Mary Burgess (s); John Humphrey (t); Luis Battle (p) (+ Casals; Mendelssohn) (Cz) Op.20

   Bedivere Records BVR 305. Beryl Tučapská (s); Carol Leatherby (mz-c); Gary Peacock (p) (+ Smetana; Foerster). (Cz) Op.32

* EMI CDH 7 69793 2. Elizabeth Schwarzkopf (s); Irmgard Seefried (s); Gerald Moore (p) (+ Monteverdi et al) (G) Op.32

   Seraphim 60376

CHILDREN'S SONG (DĚTSKÁ PÍSEŇ) (B.113) (1880). Poem by S. Bačkora

   Spectrum SR-193. Katherine Ciesinski (mz-s); Grayson Hirst (t)

RUSSIAN SONGS -- See Arrangements.

VII

Choral Songs (Part-songs)

FROM A BOUQET OF SLAVONIC FOLK-SONGS, op.43 (B.76) (1878)
1.   "Sorrow" ("Žal")
2.   "Miraculous Water" ("Divná voda")
3.   "The Girl in the Woods" ("Děvče v háji")

Everest 6164. UCLA Glee Club conducted by Donn Weiss (+ Bartók et al) in Five Centuries of Men's Choral Music. No. 1 as "Gram; No. 3 as "Maegdlein im walde." (G)

IN NATURE'S REALM, op.63 (B.126) (1882) (V PŘÍRODĚ). Five poems by Vitězslav Hálek

Supraphon 1 12 2040. Kühn Mixed Choir conducted by Pavel Kühn (+ Four Part-Songs; Novák). Complete set

Panton 8112 0383. Czechoslovak Radio Chorus conducted by Milan Malý (+ Hanuš et al) Complete set

Opus 9112 0215. Lucnica conducted by Stefan Klimo. No. 4 "The silver birch" only

RCA (Germany) PRL 1-9059

FOUR SONGS FOR MIXED CHOIR, op.29 (B.59) (1876). Nos. 1, 2 by Adolph Heyduk; Nos. 3, 4 from Moravian folk poetry
1.   "Evening's Blessing" ("Místo klekání")
2.   "Lullaby" ("Ukolébavka")
3.   "I don't say it" ("Nepovím")
4.   "The Forsaken One" ("Opuštěný")

Supraphon 1 12 2040. Kühn Mixed Choir conducted by Pavel Kühn

Most of Dvorak's part-songs owe their vitality to folk poetry and impressions of nature.   The cycle In Nature's Realm may be taken as his classic in this genre. Isolated choral songs crop up in various choral group anthologies, sometimes in German translations, but much seems to have gone unrecorded so far such as the Choral Songs for Male Voices (B.66), Bouquet of Czech Folk-Songs (B.72), Five Part-Songs for Male Voices (B.87), Hymn of the Czech Peasants (B.143), Five Lithuanian Part-Songs (B.87) and more.

VIII

Arrangements

Arrangements by Dvořák:

CYPRESSES FOR STRING QUARTET (B.152) (1887)

* ProArte CDD-237. Cleveland Quartet (+ Quartet No. 12). Complete

   Spectrum SR-196. Delos String Quartet (+ Suk). Complete

* DGG 419601. Hagen Quartet (+ Quartet No. 12). Selections

   Supraphon 50684. Dvořák Quartet (+ Quintet, op.97). Selections

* Unicorn-Kanchana DKP (CD) 9079; The English String Quartet (+ Terzetto)

TWO WALTZES FOR STRING QUARTET (B.105) (1880). (op.54, nos. 1 and 4)

   Supraphon DV 6038. Dvořák Quartet (+ Quartet No. 8) (Crossroads 22 16 0090)

* Helios CDH 88038. Delmé String Quartet (+ Hofstetter et al)

   London/Jubilee 414 143-1. Gabrieli Qt (+ Quartet No. 13)

SILENT WOODS (KLID) FOR CELLO AND PIANO (B.173) (1891).

   Supraphon 1 11 2179. Josef Suk (va); Jan Panenka (p) (+ Quintet, op.97)

   Telefunken 6.42038. Klaus Storck (vc); Karl Engel (p) in "Samtliche Werke für Violoncello und Klavier"

   Calliope CAL 1676. André Navarra (vc); Erika Kilcher (p) (+ Rondo; Humoresque; "Songs my mother..."; Fauré et al)

Also see Works for Solo Instrument and Orchestra.

SLAVONIC DANCE IN E MINOR, op.46, no. 2 arr violin and piano (B.170)

SLAVONIC DANCE IN A MAJOR, op.46, no.3, arr cello and piano

SLAVONIC DANCE IN G MINOR, op.46, no. 8, arr cello and piano (B. 172)

Supraphon MS 111 1311/12.   Josef Suk (v); Alfred Holeček (p) in "Compositions for Violin and Piano." op.46 no. 2 only

Telefunken 6.24038 AW. Klaus Storck (vc); Karl Engel (p) in "Samtliche Werke für Violoncello und Klavier." op. 46 nos. 3 and 8 only

Fritz Kreisler's transcriptions of the Slavonic Dances have enjoyed a more vigorous public life than the composer's own. The arrangement of op.46 no.3 was left uncompleted; Jarmil Burghauser reconstructed it for publication in 1973.

HUNGARIAN DANCES NOS. 17-21, Brahms orch Dvořák (B.602) (1880)

* DGG 410615-2.   Vienna Philharmonic conducted by Claudio Abbado. Complete

* Enigma Classics D21E 74630. Budapest Symphony Orchestra conducted by Bogar. Complete

* London/Weekend Classics 417 696-2. Vienna Philharmonic conducted by Fritz Reiner (+ Slavonic Dances). Nos. 5-7, 12-13, 19, 21

Brahms began to orchestrate his famous series of Hungarian Dances, but Dvořák completed the job with other arrangers appearing along the way. Anyone thirsting for more ethnic fantasies after exhausting the sixteen Slavonic Dances and ten Legends might profitably turn to Brahms-*cum*-Dvořák. Recordings are abundant.

RUSSIAN SONGS, ARR AS VOCAL DUETS WITH PIANO ACCOMPANIMENT (B.603) (c 1883). Source: M. Bernard's Pyesni ruskogo naroda

Spectrum SR-193.   Katherine Ciesinski (ms); Grayson Hirst (t); John Ostendorf (bsb); Rudolph Palmer (p) in "The Unknown Dvorak"

"The Birch Tree"

"The Country Duckling"

"Cherry-Trees"

While not an overt Russophile like Janacek, Dvořák did make a gesture of pan-Slavic sympathies by arranging sixteen Russian national songs which sound appropriately soulful. Evidently they came before Dvořák's journey to the land of the Czars, where he conducted several of his orchestral works in Moscow and St. Petersburg.

<u>Arrangements by others</u>:

(TWELVE) CYPRESSES, arr string orchestra:

    Schwann/Musica Mundi VMS 1083. RIAS Sinfonietta/Starek (+ Janáček)

THE JACOBIN: SYMPHONIC SUITE

    Urania URLP 7094. SO Radio Berlin/Kretschmar (+ <u>Carnival</u>; Smetana)

BAGATELLES, arr small orchestra or strings:

    * Musicmasters MMD 6018H. Orchester der Beethovenhalle Bonn/Dennis Russell Davies (+ <u>Bagatelles</u>; <u>Serenade</u>, op.44)

    * Campion Records RRCD 1302. Camerata Nova (+ Sextet)

SONATINA IN G MAJOR, op.100:

    A: Arr flute and piano:

        CBS M 37276. Jean-Pierre Rampal (f); John Steele Ritter (p) (+ Martinů; Feld) in "From Prague with Love"

      * RCA 7802-2. James Galway (f); Phillip Moll (p) (+ Martinů; Feld)

        Jerusalem ATD 8401. Er'ella Talmi (f); Yoav Talmi (p) (+ F.X. Mozart; Fauré; Poulenc)

    B: Arr orchestra as "Sinfonietta":

        Location Recording Service 1260 223. Isomata O/Bush (+ Hanson et al) (two LP)

    C: Arr string orchestra:

      * Campion Records RRCD 1301. Camerata Nova (+ <u>Miniatures</u>; <u>Five Dances</u>; <u>Rusalka</u> "Song to the Moon")

D: Second Movement (Larghetto) in arrangement for violin and piano by Fritz Kreisler as "Indian Lament" (sometimes "Indiana Canzonetta")

Everest 3268. Fritz Kreisler (v); V. Obrien (p) in "The Young Kreisler Violin Recital"

RCA/Victrola VIC-1472. Fritz Kreisler (v); Carl Lamson (p) in "Fritz Kreisler Souvenirs"

ASV ALH 951. Oscar Shumsky (v); Milton Kaye (p)

Telefunken 6.220032. Takako Nishizaki (v); Michael Ponti (p) in "Fritz Kreisler Edition, Vol III: Slavonic Fantasy"

*   Opus/Allegro 9351 1024. Aladar Mozi (v); Danica Mozilová (p) in "Famous Violin Miniatures"

Arr cello and piano:

*   CBS MK-37280. Yo-Yo Ma (vc); Patricia Zander (p) (+ "Songs my mother..."; Kreisler; Paganini)

MINIATURES (DROBNOSTI), op.75a

Arr string orchestra:

Supraphon 1 10 1956. Czechoslovak Chamber Orchestra, conducted by Otokar Stejskal (+ Mozart, Richter, Raats)

SLAVONIC DANCE IN E MINOR, "No. 1" arr violin/piano by Fritz Kreisler

*   Vanguard VBD-367. Mischa Elman (v); Joseph Seiger (p) in "Kreisler Favorites"

Vanguard/Everyman SRV 370 SD

*   EMI CDC 7 3767. Itzhak Perlman (v); Samuel Sanders (p) in "My Favorite Kreisler"

RCA/ Victrola VIC-1372. Fritz Kreisler (v); Carl Lamson (p) in "Fritz Kreisler souvenirs." Rec 1928

Supraphon 011 1233. Fritz Kreisler (v); Carl Lamson (p) in "The Immortal Art of Fritz Kreisler"

ASV ALH 951. Oscar Shumsky (v); Milton Kaye (p)

Telefunken 6.22032 AF. Takako Nishizaki (v); Michael Ponti (p) in "Slavonic Fantasy"

What Fritz Kreisler assembled as "Slavonic Dance No. 1" draws from two of Dvořák's originals: op.46 no. 2 and a middle section taken from op.72 no. 1. Also, the key was shifted from E Minor to G Minor and the harmony altered to produce a very free transcription.

SLAVONIC DANCE IN E MINOR, "No.2" arr violin/piano by Fritz Kreisler

* EMI CDC 7 47467-2. Itzhak Perlman (v); Samuel Sanders (p) in "My Favorite Kreisler"

* Vanguard/ Everyman VDB-367. Mischa Elman (v); Joseph Seiger (p) in "Mischa Elman Plays Kreisler Favorites"

Varese Sarabande VCDM 1000.60. Václav Hudeček (v); Josef Hála (p) in "The Devil's Trill"

ASV ALH 951. Oscar Shumsky (v); Milton Kaye (p)

Telefunken 6.220232 AF. Takako Nishizaki (v); Michael Ponti (p) in "Slavonic Fantasy"

SLAVONIC DANCE IN A-FLAT MAJOR, "No.3" arr violin/piano by Fritz Kreisler

Pearl GEMM 9324. Fritz Kreisler (v); piano accompaniment in "Fritz Kreisler Plays Encore"

RCA/ Victrola VIC-1732. Fritz Kreisler (v); Carl Lamson (p) in "Fritz Kreisler Souvenirs." Rec 1928

ASV ALH 951. Oscar Shumsky (v); Milton Kaye (p)

Telefunken 6.220032 AF. Takako Nishizaki (v); Michael Ponti (p) in "Slavonic Fantasy"

In his final pass at the Slavonic Dances Kreisler slightly shortened the piece and transposed it a half tone lower than the original.

LARGO FROM SYMPHONY NO. 9 IN E MINOR, arr violin/piano by Fritz Kreisler as "Negro Spiritual Melody"

> Varèse Sarabande VCDM 1000.60. Václav Hudeček (v); Josef Hála (p) in "The Devil's Trill"

> Telefunken 6.220032 AF. Takako Nishizaki (v); Michael Ponti (p) in "Slavonic Fantasy"

Dvořák's famous "Largo" exists in a wide variety of other arrangements, notably songs like "Goin' Home" and "Wagon Wheels."

SLAVONIC FANTASY IN B MINOR. Free adaptation of themes from Dvořák for violin and piano. Arr Fritz Kreisler

* Music and Arts Programs of America CD-286. Josef Gingold (v); Charles H. Webb (p). Rec 1976

  Vanguard VSD-71173. Mischa Elman (v); Joseph Seiger (p) in "The Art of Mischa Elman"

  ASV ALH 851. Oscar Shumsky(v); Milton Kaye (p)

  Telefunken 6.220032. Takako Nishizaki (v); Michael Ponti (p) in "Slavonic Fantasy"

SONGS MY MOTHER TAUGHT ME, op.55, No. 4. Arr for violin and piano by Fritz Kreisler

* Pearl GEMM 4324. Fritz Kreisler (v) with piano accompaniment (probably Carl Lamson) in"Fritz Kreisler Plays Encores"

* EMI CDC 7 4767-2. Itzhak Perlman (v); Samuel Sanders (p) in "My Favorite Kreisler"

* Philips 422 283-2. Arthur Grumiaux (v); István Hajdu (p) in "The Romantic Violin," Vol. II of "Famous Encores"

  ASV ALH 951. Oscar Shumsky (v); Milton Kaye (p)

* Mobile Fidelity MFCD 877. Arturo Delmoni (v); Meg Bachman Vas (p)

Arr cello and piano:

* CBS MK-37280. Yo-Yo Ma (vc); Patricia Zander (p) (+ "Indian Lament;" Kreisler; Paganini)

Other arrangements:

* CBS MK 44796. Yo-Yo Ma (vc): Patricia Zander (p) in "Portrait of Yo-Yo Ma"

* Chandos CHAN 8441. Black Dyke Mills Band conducted by Major Peter Parkes (+ "Song to the Moon" from Rusalka; band concert)

* Supraphon 32C37-7956. Josef Suk (v); Václav Hybs Orchestra conducted by Václav Hybs (+ Largo from Symphony No. 9; Chopin et al) in "Josef Suk Plays Maria"

* LaserLite 15 505. Budapest Strings in "Serenade"

   Capitol SA 8586. Capitol Symphony Orchestra conducted by Roger Wagner; Virgil Fox (o) in "Music of Reflection"

   Capitol P 8342. Hollywood Bowl Symphony Orchestra conducted by Carmen Dragon in "Gypsy!"

SYMPHONY NO. 9 IN E MINOR, "FROM THE NEW WORLD" solo guitar transcription by Kazuhito Yamshita

* RCA Victor/Red Seal 7929-2. Kazuhito Yamshita (g) (+ Stravinsky)

HUMORESQUE, op.101, No. 7 (also Humoresk) arr violin and piano by Fritz Kreisler

In an account that might not withstand scrutiny, Fritz Kreisler (then age 28) allegedly discovered Humoresque in a pile of disorganized manuscripts in Dvořák's Prague apartment near the composer's sickbed. In any event, Kriesler played this beguiling vignette so much that it became world famous. Kreisler's first recording dates from 1910, with others following down to 1938. This arrangement has become a fixture in the violinists' community, but countless other arrangements have further accrued through the years.

Vintage recordings of Kreisler performing <u>Humoresque</u> include HMV DB 314 with orchestra; Victor 74180 with George Falkenstein, piano; Victor 6692 with Carl Lamson (all 78 rpm); then into the electrical era with Franz Rupp as accompanist on Victrola 1372, reissued on LP as Victor LCT 1049. A treasury of acoustic recordings made by Kreisler between 1910-1925 was released in 1987 on LP in a five-disc boxed album issued as The Strad LB 1-5 entitled "The Art of Fritz Kreisler." Included here is a truly unique item not issued commerically: Fritz Kreisler playing <u>Humoresque</u> on the piano.

* Pearl 132 250/51. Fritz Kreisler (v) with piano accompaniment (two CD)

* Symposium Records 1045. Eugene Ysaÿe (v); Camille Decreus (p). Rec 1912

  Supraphon 1011 3193. Jan Kubelik (v) with piano accompaniment in "The Immortal Art of Jan Kubelik"

  RCA/Victrola VIC-1732. Fritz Kreisler (v); Carl Lamson (p) in "Fritz Kreisler Souvenirs"

  RCA LCT-1049. Fritz Kreisler (v); Franz Rupp (p) in "My Favorites"

  Angel 37925. Fritz Kreisler (v); Franz Rupp (p) in "Kreisler Plays Kreisler"

  Capitol L 8165. Louis Kaufman (v); Paul Ulanovsky (p) (ten-inch LP)

  Supraphon/ Master Series MS 111 1311/12. Josef Suk (v); Alfred Holeček (p) in "Antonín Dvořák: Compositions for Violin and Piano (two LP)

  * Supraphon/ Suk Treasury 11-0703-2

  Telefunken 6.220032. Takako Nishizaki (v); Michael Ponti (p) in "Slavonic Fantasy"

* Philips 420-818-2. Arthur Grumiaux (v); István Hajdu (p) in "Magic of the Violin"

* DGG/ Musikfest 413 249-2. Christian Ferras (v); Jean-Claude Amrosini (p) in "Romantic Violin"

* White Label HPC 091. Peter Csaba (v); Zoltán Kocsis (p) in "Altweiner Tanzweises und Fritz Kreisler"

  Opus 9111 0653. Aladar Mozi (v); Danica Moziová (p) in "Romantic Miniatures"

Other Arrangements:

* MCA MCAD-42211. Jascha Heifetz (v); Milton Kaye (p) in "Jascha Heifetz: The Decca Masters," Vol. I

* ASV CD DCA 624. Hideko Udagawa (v); Pavel Giliov (p) in "Heifetz Transcriptions"

* CBS M4K 42003. Isaac Stern (v); Symphony Orchestra conducted by Franz Waxman in "Celebration: Life with Music" arr Waxman (four CD)

   Columbia ML 2103. "Isaac Stern in Violin Selections from 'Humoresque'" arr Waxman. (ten-inch LP)

* Supraphon 33CO-1854. Prague Chamber Orchestra, "artistic leader" Oldřich Vlček in "Famous Encores"

* Supraphon/Treasury DC 8045 (10 1429-2 011). Prague Symphony Orchestra conducted by Václav Smetáček in "Small Czech Musical Gems"

* Pierre Verany PV-087013. Bratislava Radio Symphony Orchestra conducted by Ondrej Lenárd in "Joyaux Classiques (Jewels of the Masters)" Vol III

   Panton 8110 0319. Czech Philharmonic Orchestra conducted by Václav Neumann in "Little Pearls of Czech Classics" Rec 1983

   * Supraphon 11 0624-2

* Inak Reference Division 8705 CD. Marzhausener Accordeon Ensemble, arr Kurt Herold

   Ottavo OTR C 48609. Netherlands Brass Quintet, arr C. Hazell

   Argo ZRG 928. Philip Jones Brass Ensemble in "Romantic Brass"

* Sony SK 42175. Ensemble Wein-Berlin (+ Slavonic Dances 46/8; 72/2 et al) in "Concert a la Carte"

   Calliope 1676. André Navarra (vc); Erika Kilcher (p) (+ Rondo; Silent Woods; "Songs my mother..." et al)

   RCA LRL1 5131. James Galway (f); National Philharmonic Orchestra conducted by Charles Gerhardt in "The Magic Flute of James Galway"

   Stolat SZM 0115. Zdzislaw Piernik (tu); Lech Lesniak (p) in "Virtuoso Tuba"

* Price-Less D 20864. Pierre Fournier (vc); Concerts de Paris conducted by Jean-Marie Asberson

* EMI/Deutsche Harmonia Mundi CDC 7 47602-2. I Salonisti (+ <u>Slavonic Dance</u>, op.46 no. 1 et al) in "Humoresque"

* LaserLite 15 505. Budapest Strings (+ <u>Waltz</u>, op.54 no.2; "Songs my mother ..." in "Serenade"

* Master Digital 19 469. Budapest Strings (+ <u>Waltz</u>, op.54 no 1) in "Serenade"

  Everest/Archive of Folk and Jazz Music FS-246. Earl "Fatha" Hines (p) with jazz orchestra in "Earl 'Fatha' Hines"

  Capitol T 3241. Jack Benny (v) "ably assisted by Isaac Stern" with orchestra conducted by Izler Solomon; voice characteristics by Mel Blanc in "Jack Benny Plays The Bee"

HUMORESQUE-SWANEE RIVER, arr Richard Hayman

* RCA/Papillon 6530-2RG. Boston Pops Orchestra conducted by Arthur Fiedler (+ Symphony No. 9; <u>Carnival</u>; Enesco)

  RCA LM/LSC 2885 (+ Rose et al)

According to rumor, Dvořák took Stephen C. Foster's famous song "Old Folks at Home" (aka "Swanee River") as a model for his op. 101 no.7 Humoresque. Richard Hayman has carried the possible connection out to a delightful conclusion. In fact, Dvořák held Foster's song in such esteem that he produced his own arrangement for soprano, bass, chorus and orchestra (B.605); no recording, unfortunately, seems available.

SERENADE, op.22, arr for violin ensemble and piano by G. Saborov

* DGG/Musikfest 413 683-2. Irina Saitseva (p) with Violin Ensemble of the Bolshoi Theater conducted by Juli Reyentovich (+ "Songs my mother..." arr as "Melodia") in "Bolshoi Melodies"

  DGG 2535 326--10

WALTZ IN A, op.54 no.1, arr orchestra

* Supraphon/Treasury DC 8064 (10 1429-2 011). Prague Symphony Orchestra conducted by Václav Smetáček (+ Humoresque et al) in "Small Czech Musical Gems" arr Smetáček

* LaserLight 15 505. Budapest Strings (+ Humoresque; Songs my mother..." et al)

Addendum

Significant releases at point of publication:

* EMI CDC 7 49995-2. SYMPHONY NO. 5 IN F MAJOR; OTHELLO
  OVERTURE: SCHERZO CAPRICCIOSO. Oslo Philharmonic Orchestra
  conducted by Mariss Jansons

* Virgin Classics CD VC 790769-2. SYMPHONY NO. 5 IN F MAJOR;
  CZECH SUITE. Czech Philharmonic Orchestra conducted by Libor Pešek

* Pickwick PWK 1137. SONATINA IN G MAJOR. Vera Vaidman (v);
  Emanuel Krasovsky (p) (+ Tchaikovsky; Schubert; Kreisler) in "Romantic
  Music for Violin and Piano"

* EMI CDM 7633992. SYMPHONY NO. 8 IN G MINOR. Royal Philharmonic
  Orchestra conducted by Sir Thomas Beecham (+ Sibelius) in "Beecham
  Edition"

* Koch International/Legacy 3-7007-2. SYMPHONY NO. 7; SYMPHONY
  NO. 8. Czech Philharmonic Orchestra conducted by Václav Talich.
  Rec 1935

* Supraphon/Crystal 11 0627-2. SYMPHONY NO. 8. Czech Philharmonic
  Orchestra conducted by Václav Talich (+ Smetana). Rec 1954

* RCA/Toscanini Collection 60729-2RG (Vol 24). SYMPHONY NO. 9.
  NBC Symphony Orchestra cnoducted by Arturo Toscanini (+ Kodály;
  Smetana). Rec 1950

* Orfeo 180 891. POLONAISE IN E FLAT MAJOR; PRELUDE; FESTIVAL
  MARCH. Czech Philharmonic Orchestra conducted by Václav Neumann.
  (+ Smetana et al) in "Galakonzert aus Prag"

* BIS CD 421/424 (423). SYMPHONY NO. 6. Stockholm Philharmonic
  Orchestra, conducted by Yuri Ahronovitch; SYMPHONY NO. 7, excerpt in
  rehearsal, conducted by Antal Dorati. In "Stockholm Filharmoniske Orkester,
  75 ar 1914-1989"

* Preciosa/Aulos PRE 66002 AUL. SYMPHONY NO. 5. Bamberg Symphony
  Orchestra, conducted by Martin Turnovsky (+ Fibich)

* RCA 60234-2-RC. SYMPHONY NO. 8; SERENADE, op.22. Royal
  Philharmonic Orchestra, conducted by Claus Peter Flor

* RCA/Victrola 69135-2-RV. SLAVONIC DANCES NOS. 1, 4, 8; HUMORESQUE. Philharmonia Hungarica, conducted by Christoph von Dohnányi; Adolf Wreege and his RIAS Orchestra (+ Smetana et al) in "Humoresque"

* Chandos 8771. SEXTET. Academy of St. Martin-in-the-Fields Chamber Ensemble (+ Martinů)

* Hyperion CDA 66287. PIANO QUARTETS, op.23, 87. Domus with Susan Tomes (p)

* Music and Arts Programs of America/The Mengelberg Legacy 2058. VIOLIN CONCERTO IN A MINOR, op.53, Maria Neuss (v); Concertgebouw Orchestra conducted by Willem Mengelberg; CELLO CONCERTO IN B MINOR, op.104. Maurice Gendron (vc); Paris Radio Orchestra conducted by Willem Mengelberg

* Music and Arts Programs of America CD 658. SLAVONIC DANCES, op.46 and 72; CARNIVAL OVERTURE, op.92. Czech Philharmonic conducted by Václav Talich. Rec 1935

* London 430 171-2. SLAVONIC DANCES, op.46 and 72. The Cleveland Orchestra conducted by Christoph von Dohnányi

  Nonesuch D-79012. QUINTET IN G MAJOR, op.77; WALTZES, op.54 nos. 1 and 4. Sequoia String Quartet with Julius Levine (db). Rec 1980

  Eterna 7 29 303. BIBLICAL SONGS, op.99. Theo Adam (bba); Dresden Philharmonic conducted by Herbert Kegel (+ Martin)

* DGG 429 723-2. String Quartet No.12 "American". Emerson String Quartet (+ Smetana)

* ARS Produktion FCD 368 305. BIBLICAL SONGS. Cornelia Wulkopf (a); Klaus Schilde (p) (+ Brahms) (G)

* Supraphon 11 1430-2231. MASS IN D MAJOR (organ version); O SANCTISSIMA, op.19a; AVE MARIA, op.198; AVE MARIS STELLA, op.198; HYMNUS AD LAUDES IN FESTO SS. TRINITATIS, op.82. Soloists, organ, Czech Philharmonic Chorus, conducted by Lubomir Mátl.

* Supraphon 11 1259-2633. DIMITRIJ. Soloists, Prague Radio Chorus, Czech Philharmonic Chorus and Orchestra, conducted by Gerd Albrecht. *Complete opera*

* Telarc CD-80287. TE DEUM. Soloists; Chorus; Atlanta Symphony Orchestra, conducted by Robert Shaw (+Janáček)

Works Index

Performer Index

Abbado, Claudio, 129
Academy of St. Martin-in-the-Fields
    Chamber Ensemble, 88
Accardo, Salvatore, 74, 84, 87, 106,
    111
Adamec, Petr, 109
Ahronovitch, Yuri, 21
Alban Berg Quartet, 97
Albert (conductor), 74
Albert, Werner Andrea, 39
Albrecht, Alexander, 8
Albrecht, Gerd, 3
Alvarez Piano Quartet, 100
Amadeus Quartet, 96
Ameling, Elly, 123
American String Quartet, 91-92
Ames Piano Quartet, 100-101
Ančerl, Karel, 15, 21, 31, 44-47, 69,
    73-74
Angeles, Victoria de Los, 123
Angerer, Paul, 54
Ars Trio, 102
Ashkenazy, Vladimir, 78
Atlas, Dalia, 65
Austrian String Quartet, 84-85, 89
Ax, Emanuel, 88, 103-104

Badura-Skoda, Paul, 103, 105
Balsam, Arthur, 110, 117
Barbirolli, Sir John, 26, 37-38, 55, 61,
    67

Barchet Quartet, 99
Barenboim, Daniel, 72, 74, 77, 82
Baricova, Ljuba, 6
Bartók Quartet, 95-96, 98
Bartošová, Helena, 6-7
Barylli Quartet, 88, 98
Barzin, Leon, 81
Batiz, Enrique, 28, 36
Beaux Arts Trio, 100-102, 104
Beecham, Sir Thomas, 26 49, 66
Bělohlávek, Jiří, 64, 70, 73, 75, 79
Beňačková, Gabriela
    (Beňačkova-Čapová), 2, 4, 6, 8, 10,
    14
Benny, Jack, 137
Berger, Julius, 81
Berglund, Paavo, 43, 55, 67
Berkshire Quartet, 67, 90
Berlin Philharmonic Chamber
    Ensemble (Philharmonisches
    Kammerensemble Berlin), 68
Berlin (Philharmonic) Octet, 84,
    88-89
Berlin Philharmonic Quintet, 86
Berman, Karel, 2-3
Bernstein, Leonard, 23, 34, 36, 40, 47,
    70, 79
Beroff, Michel, 118
Bethien Quartet, 96
Bishop, Stephan, 88
Blachut, Beno, 1, 3, 14, 120-121
Blomstedt, Herbert, 29
Boettcher, Wolfgang, 112

About the Compiler

JOHN H. YOELL, a physician, is also a discographer and music publicist. He is editor of the newsletter of the Czechoslovak Music Society, a former staff contributor to *Fanfare*, and author of *The Nordic Sound*.

www.ingramcontent.com/pod-product-compliance
Lightning Source LLC
Chambersburg PA
CBHW070443100426
42812CB00004B/1196